THEY DID IT—

*Anna Marie Fisk, 36, artist—bought a $55,000 Santa Fe adobe dream house for $5,000 down and $500 per month with seller financing—and then sold it for $74,900 four years later!

*Patty Goldberg of Carmel, California, jobless—ran up bad debts a mile long before she inherited a bundle and bought a $300,000 seaside mansion with a conventional bank mortgage—using the 30/70 rule.

*Doug Starr, 25, self-employed landscaper—bought a $40,000 Missouri farmhouse with a quit claim for $5 plus his monthly mortgage payments.

*Charles Merriweather, 30ish and newly single, went from a friend's couch into a fabulous 1930s Sacramento bungalow for $550 a month and no down payment—with lease with option to buy.

YOU CAN TOO WITH—
NO CREDIT REQUIRED

NO CREDIT REQUIRED

How to Buy a House When You Don't Qualify for a Mortgage

Ray Mungo and Robert H. Yamaguchi, MBA

A SIGNET BOOK

SIGNET
Published by the Penguin Group
Penguin Books USA Inc., 375 Hudson Street,
New York, New York 10014, U.S.A.
Penguin Books Ltd, 27 Wrights Lane,
London W8 5TZ, England
Penguin Books Australia Ltd, Ringwood,
Victoria, Australia
Penguin Books Canada Ltd, 10 Alcorn Avenue,
Toronto, Ontario, Canada M4V 3B2
Penguin Books (N.Z.) Ltd, 182–190 Wairau Road,
Auckland 10, New Zealand

Penguin Books Ltd, Registered Offices:
Harmondsworth, Middlesex, England

First published by Signet, an imprint of Dutton Signet,
a division of Penguin Books USA Inc.

First Printing, April, 1993
10 9 8 7 6 5 4

 REGISTERED TRADEMARK—MARCA REGISTRADA

Printed in the United States of America

For Nancy Mayer,
author of the popular NAL book
The Male Midlife Crisis,
and our real estate guru!

DISCLAIMER

All real estate purchases involve some risk, therefore the publisher and authors cannot accept responsibility for any real estate decisions made by the reader based on information in this book. We advise all readers to use the services of professional real estate brokers and agents and, if needed, attorneys with real estate experience.

The names of the home buyers described in the book have been changed to protect their privacy, but their stories are true ones.

The authors welcome your comments on buying real estate with no credit required, and will consider them for inclusion in possible future editions. Please address them in care of the publisher.

Contents

Acknowledgments   xi

Introduction   13

1. The Government No-Qualifying
   Assumption   23

2. Home, Sweet, No-Qualifying Home   32

3. Everything About the FHA, and More   47

4. Owner Will Carry   52

5. Lease with Option   84

6. The 30/70 Rule   104

7. Adverse Possession   110

8. Equity Sharing   118

9. Foreclosure to You   130

10. Quitclaim   140

11. "En Viager," Buying From the Old,
    Dying, and Dead   145

12. The Unwanted, the Desperate,
    and the Ugly   151

13. Go for It!   160

14. Credit-Free, and Home for the Holidays   166

15. Buy It, You'll Like It   178

Glossary of Real Estate Terms   181

Index   185

ACKNOWLEDGMENTS

This book grew out of a passionate love affair with houses. The authors, separately and together, spent 20 years fixing up and restoring older homes in Vermont, Seattle, Monterey, and Palm Springs, California. The homes were in every case bought with no credit required.

The spirit of this is the philosophy that anyone, regardless of credit history, can own a home in the United States. And we sincerely believe in that American dream, which so many have lost or given up in recent years.

For particular help and invaluable advice, we thank the following: Editor Kevin Mulroy of New American Library; agent Jane Dystel; Cynthia Williams of Carmel, CA; Bob Healy and George Robbins of Morongo Valley Realty, Morongo Valley, CA; Mortgage Bankers Assn. of Washington, D.C.; Lynne Ballew of Tokai Bank, San Diego; Scott Luhrs of Century 21 Rockwell Realty, San Diego; Robert J. Bruss, syndicated real estate columnist; the cooperative and helpful staff at the Federal Housing Authority and Veterans Administration, San Diego offices; Rosie Franklin, Guilford, VT; Minnie Skinner, Seattle, WA; Tim and Brenda Asire, Morongo Valley, CA; Judy Preston of Lakeshore Terrace Realty, San Diego; J. Barney Malesky, manager of Palomar Realty, San Diego; Dr. Mitsuya Yamaguchi, Los Angeles; Rita Mungo, Lawrence, MA; and Bill and Nina Gerwin, Larkspur, CA.

Introduction

Leo Carrol's truck was stolen on a rainy night in February, and his whole credit rating went down the drain. Leo is a self-employed contractor, and the truck contained all his tools—$10,000 worth of essential implements needed to make his living disappeared along with his 1988 Dodge pickup, mobile telephone, and in-dash CD player.

Fortunately, Leo had enough credit cards to replace the truck and tools. Having no choice, he went out and charged a whole new set of working tools, made a down payment on a new Toyota, and invested in the theft insurance he should have had in the first place.

He and his wife, Teri, also decided it was time to move out of their crime-ridden neighborhood of Atlanta and buy a house in some pleasant, family-oriented suburb. Teri was pregnant with their first child.

Alas, the truck and tools replacement pushed Leo and Teri into uncontrollable debt. The Visa and MasterCard bills got paid later and later until one month, one big job didn't come through (the real estate developer who had hired Leo went bankrupt), and they couldn't make any payment at all. The usurious 18 percent interest rate increased their indebtedness faster than they could keep up, bill collectors began calling at all hours, and black marks of delinquency cropped up all over their credit rating.

The hardworking couple needed a home but had lost any hope of being able to qualify for a mortgage. Their landlord was a "jerk" (Leo's term) who raised the rent every six months while refusing to do repairs or provide services, and they were determined not to bring a child into the world in their rundown rental unit.

They'd just about given up, and Teri was crying herself to sleep every night, when they noticed the advertisement in a weekly throwaway newspaper. "$3,000 moves you in," it read. "Lease with option to buy. Older two-story home with yard, close to schools and shopping. $750 rent applies to purchase. No credit required. Open house Sunday, 1–4 P.M."

They drove out to see this impossible bargain. It was located in a small town on a pretty lake, a half-hour's commute time to Teri's job at the Atlanta airport, where she was a clerk for a car-rental company. Leo already drove all over the county doing his work, so the distance didn't bother him. At a sale price of $79,900, this house was everything the Carrols ever wanted in a home. It was in passably good condition and had an enormous backyard with an old oak tree equipped with a rope swing and nifty treehouse.

The owners were a conservative older couple. The husband, a sales representative for a major pharmaceuticals company, had been transferred from Atlanta to the Tallahassee office. In the wake of the 1990s recession, these folks had found it impossible to sell their home, and after listing it for six months with no offers, they decided to try the lease option route. Anything was preferable to paying rent ($795) on their new home in Tallahassee and also meeting mortgage payments ($610) on their empty house in Georgia.

Leo and Teri knew they wanted the house, but in addition to having no credit they didn't have the $3,000 down payment (nonrefundable option fee) to get in. But Leo's a good talker, and he persuaded the owners to give him two weeks to come up with the money. Then he went out and worked like a maniac, night and day, and even cajoled one client to pay him in advance. Right on schedule, the Carrols produced a cashier's check for $3,750 (the option fee, plus first month's rent) and moved into their dream home with a few nasty parting words to their jerk landlord.

Within the first ten months of their lease, Leo and Teri found they had accumulated an astonishing $10,500 equity in their home—$7,500 in rent applied to purchase, plus the original $3,000 down—and owed only $69,400 on the house. They also had a 9-pound, 3-ounce baby boy named after Leo's grandfather, Max. To boot, they discovered six months into their lease that the previous owner's mortgage was an assumable Federal Housing Administration (FHA) with "no qualifying" type, which they could take over for a mere $45 transfer fee. The old mortgage balance was at $59,000, so they needed only $10,400 to buy the house.

Grandpa Max came through with about $6,500, saying it was probably the best thing he could do for his new grandson and namesake and that he "couldn't take it with me, anyway." Leo had been working hard and had paid on his credit card bills to the point of being able to scrape up the remaining $4,000 or so.

Voilà, before their 12-month lease option had expired, the Carrols had managed to buy the house even though they never did acquire enough credit to qualify for a mortgage. They also conceived a second child, expected to be a girl. The previous owners got about ten grand in rent and another ten grand at the closing of escrow, and were happy as could be. And, when they assumed the old mortgage, Leo and Teri saw their monthly payment drop from $750 to about $610. It was actually cheaper to own the house than to rent it!

The tax advantages were stupendous, also. For the first time in his life, Leo could deduct mortgage interest and real estate taxes from his taxable income, and Teri got every cent of the withholding tax from her job in a whopping refund.

Owning the house seemed to improve the Carrols' credit rating overnight. They were deluged with home equity loan offers by mail. If they pay their mortgage on time for a few years, there's no question they will eventually be able to qualify for a new mortgage on a newer and more expensive home. But they didn't need one scrap of credit to become first-time homeowners. And neither do you!

No Credit, No Job, No Problem

No kidding! The Carrols' story is just one of many examples of how people lacking the credit to qualify for a mortgage can nonetheless buy a home. Leo and Teri are not even close to an extreme case. Plenty of folks have bought property while having no credit at all, terrible credit with a history of bankruptcy or delinquency, no job of any kind, or even a criminal record.

You can do it, too. It takes a bit of patience to find the right home, the right deal and terms. Some of these homes are available for "nothing down" as well, but this book is not focused on those rare properties. In truth, you can't buy a house without needing money—usually there will be a down payment of some kind, and there is always a monthly mortgage payment, but if you are a reasonable person who is now paying rent and somebody in your family has an income (not necessarily from a steady job), you can almost certainly buy a home *regardless of how bad or nonexistent your credit is*.

And there has never been a better or easier time to buy without credit. Everybody knows the recession of the 1990s has put a severe crimp into the real estate industry. Prices are going down, terms are getting more liberal, sellers are desperate and willing to consider creative financing that would have been unthinkable a few years back. You can take advantage of these market conditions and survive the recession quite well in a home of your own that will rebound in value when the economy improves.

Not having good credit doesn't make you a bad person, and there's no reason to feel ashamed or reluctant to shop for a home. The nation as a whole is in a "credit crunch" right now, with bad real estate loans leading the pack of factors that brought on the savings and loan crisis. The banks' persistent marketing of credit cards had put a lot of us in debt over our heads. Big companies have been laying off thousands of workers, honest people who counted on their jobs to pay their bills and who now see their credit ratings plummet as their paychecks vanish. The entire housing industry has to adjust to these conditions. You are in step with the times if your credit is lousy!

The computer age has made it all but impossible to hide your bad credit, so you need to restrict your house hunting to deals that are explicitly "no credit required." Don't even waste your time and the real estate agent's efforts on property that requires you to "qualify." Be honest and tell that agent up front what you need. Better yet, show him or her this book. You'll find a high percentage of agents and brokers don't know much about these deals, and some are reluctant to learn. They're caught in a mind-set of earning their commission, typically 6 percent of the sale price, and want to deal with buyers who can command a big mortgage payout from a bank or other commercial lender. But in uncertain times like these, you may be able to educate your agent about unconventional ways to buy.

Of course, there are limitations and rules to follow. You can't really expect to purchase a millionaire's mansion with no credit, but you'd be surprised at what is possible. Here in California, we've seen half-million dollar homes advertised as "no qualifying," the magic phrase that opens the door.

Take a look at your current situation. How much do you pay in rent in a year? Whatever it is, it's money thrown in the gutter in the sense that you'll never own a stick or nail of your home no matter how many years you pay. If you've lived in the same place for a long time, you may even have already paid what the house once cost. Most parts of the nation saw a dramatic increase in home values during the 1970s and 1980s. Your landlords have reaped the benefit as well as all the tax advantages, while all you get is the right to occupy the premises for 30 days at a time.

Now look at the real estate prices in your neighborhood—and if they are too high, look around at other neighborhoods. Buying without credit may force you to move to a less desirable part of town, or to take on a house that needs work, or to share equity with another investor. We'll discuss all the possibilities in this book. For now, figure out what you can afford to pay every month and look for something in that range. Most people will find that they can actually own a home for no more per month than they are already paying in rent. As a general rule of thumb, the mortgage payment should be about 1 percent of the mortgage balance—so if you're carrying $80,000, you'd pay $800 a month.

This is only a general rule, remember. It all depends on the interest rate of the mortgage. Rates are declining in the 1990s, but they fluctuate with the market. You want an interest rate under 10 percent if possible, and you prefer a fixed rate to an "adjustable," changing one.

Don't limit your house search to places that are actively advertising themselves as "no qualifying." Few do. But many times a seller who hasn't been able to unload his or her home may be open to a no-credit suggestion. A house for sale may be available for lease option if you present the seller with an attractive offer. Many sellers can be persuaded to carry the financing themselves, with the house itself serving as collateral, especially if the home has defects or problems that would cause a bank to refuse to issue a mortgage. A house that's advertised for rent may be for sale under the right circumstances. Use your imagination, and don't be afraid. The possibilities are endless.

Here are some of those endless possibilities. Every one of these will be covered in greater length in this book, and we'll illustrate them with true stories of homeowners who succeeded. But just for a quick thumbnail sketch, you can buy property without credit in any combination of the following ways:

• **The no-qualifying, assumable government mortgage.** These federal mortgages are issued by the Federal Housing Administration (FHA) and Department of Veterans Affairs (VA). The original holder of the mortgage must pass a credit test, but the loan can be passed on to succeeding owners without even filling out a credit application. We'll tell you all the rules and limits and where to find these deals.

• **Seller financing, or "owner will carry."** This is the most typical way that people buy real estate without bank approval, and it's more popular than ever these days. The seller extends financing to the buyer and "carries" the mortgage on a private real estate contract. If the buyer fails to pay the mortgage payments, the seller can take the property back and the buyer loses everything he's put into it. You can approach a seller with a proposal of owner financing in a convincing way, so that even a seller who hasn't considered the service may consent.

• **Lease with option.** You can get into a lease option purchase for a very modest amount of money and with no credit required. We offer tips and life experiences about turning a lease option over into a title deed. We advise scouring the listings in search of vacant property or property that's been languishing in a slow market, cases where the seller might be relieved to have income from the house and the buyer gradually builds equity while renting.

• **The 30/70 rule.** This is a rule you won't find written down at any lending institution, but it's a common practice. A buyer who can put down 30 percent of the sale price of a house can usually get a loan for the 70 percent balance, regardless of credit. The reasoning is that anyone who pays 30 percent into a house is highly unlikely to walk away from the investment.

• **Adverse possession.** In most states, you can gain legal title to property without credit or even payments by "open and hostile" occupation of the premises. You must file adverse possession papers and take every measure to inform the rightful owner of your intentions and presence. This is a kind of legal squatting that concludes in taking title.

• **Equity sharing.** This relatively new idea has become very popular as real estate soared beyond the reach of many people in the affluent 1980s. One party may put up the down payment and credit, while the other invests sweat and remodeling labor; or there could be a shared living arrangement, group purchase, or time-share plan. The advantage to the buyer without good credit is that equity sharing provides a start in home ownership, a foot in the door.

• **Foreclosure to you.** Foreclosure sales are way up in this distressed economy, and a professional investor with ready cash can scoop up a real bargain. The foreclosure specialist then offers the house for sale at a modest down payment, with a mortgage as long as 40 years at high interest. The only person you have to convince of your creditworthiness is the foreclosure shark him(her)self, and these deals frequently require no credit at all.

• **Quitclaim.** One of the most common and easy ways to buy without credit is to buy in joint tenancy with a relative or friend who has good credit, and have that person then quitclaim (grant) the deed to you. The original buyer's good credit remains on the line, however, which can lead to a disastrous strain on personal relationships if the payments fall behind. Quitclaiming works fine as long as trust prevails, and many a first-time buyer gets this kind of help from a parent or close friend.

• **"En viager."**   This is a chapter about obtaining property from the elderly or the deceased. It isn't limited to inheritance. The French have a system called "en viager" in which the property changes hands but the elderly person retains a lifetime right to occupancy. In the United States, we have life estate grants, reverse mortgages, estate liquidation sales to settle probate, and emergency sales to pay death taxes. This doesn't have to be a grim business. After all, they couldn't take it with them, and you may be the beneficiary of a no-credit transaction.

• **The unwanted, the desperate, and the ugly.** How to find "property in trouble," situations where the real estate is hard to sell and therefore no credit is required to buy it. Many decent houses are virtually given away by desperate sellers who have to leave them for personal reasons, and sometimes a dilapidated fixer-upper can be a great investment. Unwanted property also includes government repos, vacant houses in declining urban neighborhoods, and homes abandoned in depressed rural areas.

• **Go for it!**   Even if you have no credit, you can have your own piece of the rock if you want it badly enough, work for it, and keep it up. We'll tell you how. Read on.

CHAPTER ONE

The Government No-Qualifying Assumption

The day we bought the house (August 15, 1989), neither of us had a job. Our combined savings were nothing great. And neither of us had a credit rating good enough to qualify for a mortgage. But in a matter of 15 minutes, for $500 in earnest money, we bought a modern home with swimming pool, hot tub, garage, and walled yard near Palm Springs, California, and simply assumed the previous owner's mortgage. We never even filled out a credit application.

"Make sure to tell the sellers that one of us is a published author and the other a college professor," we instructed the real estate agent who wrote up the purchase offer. "We're quite respectable."

"That's what *you* say, I don't know," the agent said, laughing. "Hell, anybody can assume this mortgage for the $45 transfer fee. It doesn't matter whether you're respectable or not!"

And it didn't matter that we were unemployed, or had credit problems in our pasts. It didn't matter because it was irrelevant. This gorgeous house, like thousands of others in the United States, was covered by a Federal Housing Authority (FHA) mortgage, and the bank knew that if the owner fell into default, the government would have to pay off the loan. Guaranteed by law.

This particular mortgage was subject to "automatic assumption with no qualifying." Translation:

no credit required, period! Even if you can't get a Visa or MasterCharge card, have been bankrupt, just got out of jail, or are living on unemployment or disability checks, you can still own your own home and stop paying rent.

Considering how simple it is to assume an FHA mortgage without having to qualify for the loan, it's amazing that so few real estate brokers advise home buyers of the possibility!

Admittedly, there is a limit to the amount of mortgage you can assume: $124,875 for a single-family house, or $124,850 for a condominium (1991 figures). If you live in an area of the country where single-family homes average $200,000 or more, the FHA assumption may be less than what you need, although you can still assume the mortgage if you can find some way to pay the difference. In most parts of the United States, however, the median price of a home is still within that $124,875 limit.

And, in many states, it's going down!

It also makes a big difference when the original mortgage was written. If the original loan application was signed prior to December 1, 1986, there are no restrictions. That's right, *every* FHA mortgage issued on a single-family home (or condo) before December 1986 is, in the FHA's own language, "fully assumable by owner and non-owner occupants (investors) with no acceleration of mortgage." You don't even have to occupy the home yourself to take over the mortgage without credit or qualifying.

Furthermore, the bank or lending company is prohibited by law from refusing to transfer the mortgage to any buyer.

The only other hitch to this plan is that in most cases the seller's good credit remains liable for the mortgage for a five-year period in the event that you, the buyer, should fail to make your payments or go into default.

If you don't pay the mortgage, you will certainly be foreclosed upon, and lose the property to the bank or mortgage company that holds the loan. Under these circumstances, your inadequate credit rating will get even worse, and the person(s) who sold to you may suffer a bad report on their own credit rating if they don't take over the payments.

It's possible that the seller could even get the property back after the new owner defaults, in which case he or she could reap a huge profit, because the defaulting buyer would lose every cent paid into the house.

There are a thousand different scenarios that could conceivably take place in the event of default or foreclosure, and the contract between seller and buyer will influence the outcome. But generally speaking, with a no-qualifying assumption, the seller really can't lose in the long run, and the buyer gets the property easily—and quickly! This simple assumption without bank qualifying can close escrow in a matter of a few days or weeks.

The seller has the option of getting a "release of liability processed under the 2210 procedure" (more government lingo) but only if "the credit of the purchaser has been approved by the department of Housing and Urban Development or a Direct Endorsement (DE) lender." Skip it. If the seller insists that your credit be approved, then it's not a no-credit transaction and you're not interested. In order for you to take possession without qualifying, the seller must be willing to take the risk that you are going to keep up the payments for at least five years, although you have every right to resell the house within that time.

In fact, the beauty of the December 1986-or-earlier

FHA mortgage is that you, too, can pass it along to the next buyer with no credit, as long as you've owned the home for at least one year.

After December 1986, the FHA rules changed, but there is still a "window of opportunity" there for no-credit purchasing. If the mortgage was issued between December 1, 1986 and December 14, 1989, the FHA states that "all (such) mortgages require a credit-worthiness review of each person who seeks to assume the mortgage *during the first 12 months after execution if the original mortgagor was an owner-occupant, or during the first 24 months after execution if the mortgagor was an investor.*" In other words, you as the buyer have one or two years in which to pass the credit test. Even if your credit isn't good enough when you buy the house, you'd still be in the clear as long as it improved enough in that year or two to pass a credit review.

FHA mortgages issued after December 15, 1989 drop the no-qualifying provision altogether. You have to pass a creditworthiness review in order to assume one of these newer loans. In today's increasingly troubled economy, with defaults and foreclosures sharply on the rise, the FHA has become much more demanding about who can assume a mortgage.

Find a house or condo with an FHA mortgage issued prior to December 1986, then, and you could be an instant homeowner even if you're a lifelong deadbeat!

How to Find an FHA Assumable Mortgage

We mentioned earlier that few real estate brokers advise home buyers of the possibility of assuming a no-qualifying FHA mortgage. There is no reason for an agent or broker to shy away from these mortgages, however. Indeed, they are a real estate gold mine to the agent as well as the buyer. Why, then, don't agents and brokers push these easy assumables?

The simple answer is that many of them don't even know about this government boon—especially agents who got into the business after December 1986. Even those who are aware of the rule don't know which houses carry the right kind of assumable mortgage. The FHA itself will not release to the public the addresses of homes it has mortgaged, and it does not keep records of the transfers when one owner lets the next owner assume the loan. Because the mortgages are issued by regular banks and S&Ls or mortgage companies, but are **guaranteed** and backed by the FHA, the FHA doesn't even learn of the transfer unless the new owner falls into default.

So, how do you find an FHA assumable mortgage? It's easy.

1. Ask! Ask the agent, or the seller, "Does the house have an FHA mortgage, and is it assumable with no qualifying?" Was the FHA mortgage issued prior to December 1, 1986? If so, you're in. If not, don't despair. Millions of other houses have the right kind of FHA mortgage.

2. Direct the agent or broker to search the listings for houses with assumable mortgages. In this age of computers, it's easily done in most parts of the country. Most multiple listings will address the question: Mortgage: Assumable? Y or N (for "yes" or "no"). Once you have located the houses with assumable mortgages in your price range and desired location, narrow the search further to which of those mortgages are FHA ones from December 1, 1986, or earlier.

There is an important distinction between assumable mortgages. Some are just regular mortgages from a bank, and they are assumable, but you still have to pass a credit test. The only no-credit assumptions are either from the FHA or the Department of Veterans Affairs (see below).

3. Scan the homes for sale classified listings, hunting for the magic words "FHA/VA assumable" or "no qualifying." Depending on what part of the country you live in, such listings could be scarce. They will never constitute more than a small percentage of the total number of ads in the paper. Remember that many listings with FHA assumable mortgages don't bother to include that fact in the ad. But, when you see "no qual." or "FHA assum." in an ad, you've found a seller you can work with!

4. Inquire, ask around, be specific. Remember the FHA is the single largest guarantor of home mortgages in the nation. Very expensive homes don't qualify, but middle-class homes in every part of the country are covered by these FHA-backed loans.

What Is an "Assumable" Mortgage?

An "assumable" mortgage is simply one that you, the buyer, can take over. You make the previous owner's payments. The term of the loan, the amount owed, the interest rate (if it's a fixed one), don't change. Owner A simply allows Owner B to take over his or her payments.

For example, if the seller was paying $576 a month on a balance of $60,000 owed on the house, you will pay the same amount and owe the same amount. If the mortgage was a 30-year loan with 6 years already paid and 24 years to go, you'll have the same

24 years to go. Nothing about the mortgage changes except the person who is paying it.

There is always a fee of some kind for the service of transferring the mortgage to a new owner's name. With the FHA no-qualifying mortgage, the transfer fee is quite modest, only $45 in 1991.

There is nothing particularly complicated about this assumption—that's the beauty of it. Naturally, you should have title to the property transferred in a proper and legal fashion, handled by a reputable escrow company, and duly recorded in county records. The bank or lending institution will then begin mailing payment coupons or statements to you as the new owner of the home.

The escrow office is what keeps us all honest. Essentially, an escrow company holds money and legal documents and distributes them to their rightful owners at the time of closing. Of course, the escrow office charges a fee for this service, included in the "closing costs." A very sharp seller will sometimes ask the buyer to pay half the escrow fees, but usually it's the seller's responsibility to meet the closing costs. When the escrow company closes the deal, the buyer gets the deed to the house (Title), the seller gets the money coming to him, and the company records the transfer with the county recorder.

You don't absolutely need an escrow company to handle all this paperwork and monetary exchange, but we don't recommend trying a do-it yourself job unless you're very experienced. There is just too much at stake to take a chance on errors. The escrow company is insured to cover mistakes, whereas you are not.

The VA Mortgage—Whether or Not You're a Veteran

The Federal Department of Veterans Affairs (VA) also provides help in purchasing a home if you have served in the armed forces. Veterans can often buy with no down payment, as well. And the VA mortgage can be assumed with absolutely no qualifying and no credit, **regardless of whether or not the buyer is a veteran**, as long as the original VA loan was made before March 1, 1988. But the rules are different from FHA as follows:

1. The government issues the veteran a Certificate of Eligibility, which says to the bank or mortgage lender that 25 percent of the loan is guaranteed up to a maximum of $46,000, meaning the home price must be $184,000 or less, or the veteran must make up the difference. The vet must also qualify for income and credit.

2. The original loan must have closed prior to March 1, 1988 in order for the mortgage to be assumable with no qualifying. VA loans made after that date require the buyer to be qualified by the lending institution, so it's not a no-credit situation.

3. When a veteran sells property to someone who assumes an existing VA loan, the veteran is not automatically released from personal liability for repayment of the loan. As long as it dates from before March 1, 1988, the mortgage can be assumed without any approval from the VA or the lender, *but* (and these are the VA's own words) "the veteran is strongly urged to request a release of liability from VA."

4. If the veteran does not obtain a release of liability, he or she could be responsible for the debt if

the buyer quits making payments or falls into default, and there is no five-year limit to the responsibility. As stated in the government literature, "strenuous collection efforts will be made against the veteran if a debt is established." For this reason, a lot of vets are naturally reluctant to let a buyer assume their loan. When you assume a VA loan without qualifying and without a release of liability for the seller, you are literally assuming that seller's good credit—indefinitely.

5. In order to get a release of liability, the vet must have the VA or the lender approve the buyer and the assumption, so you as buyer must have credit.

If these VA rules seem somewhat tighter and more stringent than the FHA ones, don't let it discourage you! All it comes down to is that you have to convince the seller, not any bank or government agency, to trust you to make the payments, and if that seller wants or needs to sell the house badly enough, he or she WILL let you assume the loan. Millions of homes are guaranteed by VA loans, and thousands of these no-qualifying assumptions are recorded every year.

Just as with the FHA assumption, the veteran could retrieve the property if the buyer goes into default, but naturally no seller wants to encounter problems. You can help your own cause by demonstrating to that vet, in writing, your ability to make the mortgage payment. List your assets, the amount your household earns from jobs, and produce copies of your past years' IRS returns.

There really isn't that much for the vet to fear if you are able to meet the mortgage payment. Remember, you should never buy any property with a mortgage payment higher than you can meet! So don't be afraid. Assume and prosper!

CHAPTER TWO

Home, Sweet
No-Qualifying Home

In the spring of 1989, the average first-time home buyers in California needed Grade A credit, a down payment of $30,000, and a household income of $85,000 a year, according to a syndicated newspaper story. In our (nontraditional) family, we had the opposite: credit problems in the past, savings well under $10,000, and a household income that fluctuated wildly. Neither of us had a full-time job. Yet we passionately wanted to own a home. After years of renting houses on the Monterey coast, we'd already paid more than what some of those houses once cost, but had nothing to show for our investment.

We had purchased real estate without having or needing any credit nine times in the past, however, so we knew it could be done, even while legions of so-called experts and real estate lenders said, essentially, "forget it." Without an excellent credit rating and a stable, long-term job, nobody can afford to buy a house, it was commonly believed. Not in California, at any rate, and not in the feverish boom market of the late 1980s. We were discouraged, but we never gave up.

The Federal Housing Administration (FHA) assumable mortgages described in the previous chapter are obviously perfect for buyers in our situation—people who have some money to put down and the ability to pay a reasonable monthly amount, but no quali-fying credentials.

The Monterey Peninsula wasn't the best place to find such a deal, however. The area is a coastal par-adise, tourist retreat, and haven for affluent retired folks. Actor Clint Eastwood's stint as mayor of Car-mel, with its attendant worldwide publicity, just ex-acerbated the problem of overcrowded beaches and spiraling values. Eastwood himself is a major land-holder in the Carmel area, and he virtually admitted that he ran for mayor of Carmel primarily out of frustration that the city council would not grant him permits to expand and improve his properties.

From 1980 to 1990, the price of a typical house in the Monterey-Carmel-Pebble Beach region multi-plied many times over, soaring out of control. So, even if you could find an automatic assumption, the mortgage balance was much lower than the asking price—meaning you had to come up with a huge down payment or ask the seller to extend financing for a second Deed of Trust (essentially, a second mortgage and added monthly payment).

Look at what happened to Abbie Lou Williams's rental cottages by the sea in neighboring Pacific Grove. Abbie Lou, a Carmel artist and local gallery owner in her seventies, crashed her Volvo into a tree and died in 1984, on the same month and day that her husband had perished in a car crash ten years earlier. Abbie Lou was a strong-willed and fiercely health-conscious individual who had not concluded making arrangements for her own demise. In partic-ular, she had not deeded her rental houses to her children or protected them from probate.

Following the tragic accident, her distraught heirs were quickly forced to sell off some of her rentals to raise money for the taxes. Some lucky person just assumed the $77,500 mortgage on a nice corner-lot home, then resold the place five years later for $243,000. To buy the house without credit now, you'd need at least $166,000 in cash to make up the difference between the mortgage balance and the price tag.

With Carmel fixer-uppers going for $300,000 to $400,000, we soon realized that we had to look for a more humble community in order to buy a house without credit. We scoured around all the little farm towns of northern California—barely missed investing in Watsonville just months before the devastating October 1989 earthquake. But we wound up buying a house in the high desert town of Morongo Valley, 17 miles from Palm Springs, a place we fell in love with, a cushy mountain retreat with swimming pool, hot tub, and all the amenities. The price was $69,000, the down payment $7,000, the monthly mortgage $557 (including taxes and insurance). We went into escrow with a $500 "earnest money" deposit and owned the place three weeks later.

This "Palm Springs Palace" fit our needs and qualifications exactly. After looking at dozens of other houses in that area, we had decided that we wanted: (1) a modern home with at least three bedrooms; (2) a swimming pool and central air-conditioning for the hot summers; (3) a Jacuzzi or spa to soothe aching 45-year-old joints; (4) absolute privacy in the backyard; (5) scenic views a plus; and (6) a place that cost *no more than $7,000 down, with no credit required, and a monthly payment under $1,000*. Other houses had come close to meeting our practically impossible criteria, but this house met them all.

The price was $69,000, the FHA automatic assumption mortgage balance about $59,000, meaning the sellers had only about $10,000 coming to them—out of which they had the agent's commission of about $4,200. We had only $7,000 to put down, so the sellers agreed to "carry" the remaining $3,000 for one year at 10 percent interest, and a year later we cashed them out. All things considered, they didn't make much money from selling the place, but they'd already moved anyway, and were desperate to get rid of it when we stumbled on the scene on a hot August day.

The house was built in 1974 by a swimming pool contractor and his wife, who put in the 20- by 40-foot Olympic-style pool, the hot tub, the lush green lawn (6 inches deep landfill of topsoil imported from somewhere other than the high desert, which is only sand), the palm trees, the adobe brick walls, two-car garage addition, and family den room with Western beams and yippie-eye-oh-ky-yay cowboy motifs. The second set of owners were proprietors of the leading paint and wallpaper retail outlet in ritzy Palm Desert, and they did all the floors, walls, and ceilings in designer colors with the most expensive materials left over from custom jobs. Our Japanese grass wallpaper, we were told, came from the selection of Joan Kroc, widow of Ray Kroc, founder of McDonald's. The master bathroom is wallpapered in flecked, hand-painted foil. We redid the landscaping, interior decoration, new guest bedroom, new formal dining room, sun porch room, and other nice touches.

But the place was in sad condition on the day we found it. The swimming pool was nothing more than an empty hole in the ground, filthy from evaporation and blown sand and neglect. The hot tub was black with soot and dust. Vandals had stolen the motors for the pool and spa filters. The lawn was yellow thatch of dead straw. For six months, while an apparent sale deal went sour and died, the house had stood empty and vulnerable, its owners installed in their new residence.

Our little desert town (pop. 1,300 and constantly

growing) decided to build a new elementary school directly across the street from the house, so for the first year we woke up very, very early each Monday through Friday morning to a crashing symphony of bulldozers, cranes, jackhammers, huge trucks, and crews of hirsute workers with ear-shattering boom-box radios. Once the school opened for "business," we woke to the roar of fat yellow school buses, parents' cars and trucks, and hundreds of shrieking children, but not before 8 A.M., thank goodness, and not during weekends, holidays, or summers.

The first couple of months in the house were nerve-racking. Could it be we really owned this place and the Bank of America really sent us a mortgage payment coupon at $557 a month, without even asking for a credit rating or proof of a job? Indeed it was true. But home ownership led to unanticipated expenses, of course. A pool service man calmly handed us a bill for $800 for two afternoons' attention to our private lake, an electrician discovered the wiring to the pool needed replacement, a spa repairman casually remarked on our underground leak, the roof suddenly started leaking when the first rains came. You get the picture. The $557 a month bargain really cost a couple of thousand dollars a month by the time we paid all the utilities, water, power, gas, roof work, driveway paving, landscaping, sprinkler system, underground drip irrigation, heat in the winter, cooling in the summer, gas and maintenance costs driving 20 to 40 miles each way daily across the howling lonesome desert to get to a (newfound, and necessary) job in Palm Springs or Palm Desert, fencing, septic upkeep, long-distance phone bills (every call is long distance when you live in Morongo Valley), and vastly increased cost of basic foodstuffs and supplies from small mom and pop merchants and a local convenience store, in the absence of major supermarkets and shopping malls.

Ah, the bucolic life.

Despite all the expenses, the house provided a much higher standard of living than any rental cottage in Monterey, plus the almost amazing benefit of substantial deductions on income tax liability. More than 90 percent of the mortgage payment is interest, and deductible, which means that Uncle Sam is literally helping to pay for the house. Moving expenses, capital improvements, home repairs, and additions made to the property in order to sell it also provide tax breaks, and you're allowed to make any amount of profit on selling your home with no taxes due at all, as long as you purchase another principal residence of equal or greater value within 24 months. Talk about encouragement! The government has stacked the deck in favor of homeowners and against renters. These tax benefits are so generous that some investors will finance a home purchase in partnership with a co-owner/occupant in order to share in the tax writeoffs (see Chapter Eight, "Equity Sharing").

Considering that absolutely no credit was needed to buy the house, it's amusing to discover how much credit merely owning one seems to give you! Within days of closing escrow and filing our deed with San Bernardino County, we started receiving come-ons and pitches in the mail offering home equity loans, home improvement loans, credit cards, instant cash, you-already-qualify scams, all kinds of insurance, every imaginable scheme to get the homeowner deeper into debt. These loans and lines of credit are based on the house itself as collateral, of course. You may be a former deadbeat with a sordid history of credit card delinquency, but if you own a home you can probably borrow against it, up to a point. Check out the story of Denise Morton and her Marine husband, Jim:

A Cautionary No-Credit Tale

When they first moved to San Diego from North Carolina, the Mortons were delighted to find that they could afford to own a home without credit. Jim's military pay from Camp Pendleton and Denise's income from part-time work as an intern for a speech therapist were enough to swing the $860 a month payment on a cute little peaked-roof Victorian-style home they bought for $90,000 in 1988. Denise's mother loaned them $5,000 for the down payment, and they simply assumed the FHA no-qualifying mortgage of $85,000.

The house was small, but it had real potential. It had two bedrooms and one bath (one of the bedrooms was tiny, and they used it as a television viewing room), a separate single-car garage, and some nice quality features such as tile work, stone steps, a living-room fireplace, built-in cabinets, hardwood floors, glass doorknobs. (It was the glass doorknobs that pushed Denise into buying the place. She was crazy about everything from the fifties, and had fantasies of restoring the house to its original look, including authentic period furniture and appliances.) It was located on a corner lot with a front yard, plenty of room to add on another bedroom and bath someday.

The neighborhood (North Park) isn't the best in San Diego, but it's not the worst either. It's close to San Diego State University, but unfortunately also close to topless dancer bars, an assortment of pawn shops, and some taco stands straight out of Tijuana.

A mixed neighborhood of well-tended "pride of ownership" homes alongside squalid rentals and blocky apartment slabs, this area is politely called a "transition zone" by the real estate agents—meaning it is in the middle of a racially mixed neighborhood. On one side is trendy Hillcrest with its Uptown urban renewal project and chic restaurants, and on the other lies City Heights, a rundown ghetto of constant police sirens and lives shattered by crack cocaine.

Jim and Denise enjoyed their home, even if it seemed to eat up all their earnings every month. They never got around to restoring the place because it was all they could do to pay the mortgage, insurance, taxes, utilities, occasional repairs, and routine upkeep. The stone fireplace was their special price and joy. Almost every night after dinner (spaghetti, usually), they sat on a battered old sofa in front of the fireplace eating popcorn, talking about all the things they'd do to improve the house if they could only afford it, about Denise's plan to get a master's degree and hence a better job as a speech therapist, and then in five years Jim would retire from the Marines and they'd start having children.

When the letter from Fidelity Home Improvement of San Diego arrived, the offer seemed too good to pass up. The outside of the envelope boldly announced in red ink, "**JIM AND DENISE MORTON,** you have already qualified for **$10,000 CASH** to improve your home!" Just another unsolicited advertisement, Jim thought, and as he was about to toss it into the fireplace, Denise retrieved it. The credit application form inside was already filled out with their names, their address, their mortgage loan number; all they had to do was sign the document and return it in the postpaid reply envelope—and after a brief discussion, that's exactly what they did. They figured they'd use the loan to fix up the house, then sell it for a good solid profit in the booming San Diego real estate market.

Fidelity Home Improvement sent them some additional forms to sign—essentially placing a lien on title to the house as collateral for the loan. They had to pay a "loan processing fee" of $50, and $10 to a notary public to certify their signatures. But Fidelity H.I. never even phoned the Mortons, and just like that a $10,000 check arrived in their mailbox in early 1990.

Jim was ecstatic. He decided to refurbish the garage into a woodworking shop. Denise planned to go ahead with her fifties restoration idea. They celebrated by inviting all their friends from the Marine base for a rollicking barbeque with plenty of steaks and an ocean of keg beer, and Jim finally bought new tires for his old pickup truck.

Within a week, the first $500 of the $10,000 was spent, but the young couple hadn't begun their home improvement work. They started in the bathroom, replacing the "grody" old wallpaper with seashell-colored tiles. They installed glass doors on the fireplace. And they shored up a part of the kitchen floor that had been sloping and rotting out. But there was never enough time to take on the really big remodeling jobs, and every week or two some financial emergency arose—dentist bills, carburetor work, washing machine repair—and, little by little the $10,000 evaporated. Toward the end, they used the loan money to make the mortgage payment one month. In addition to that $860 obligation, they now had a payment on their home improvement loan, so their monthly minimum cost had risen well over a thousand dollars, but the house was not substantially improved. The garage remained an old, leaky structure, not a woodworking shop. The house wasn't a lovingly restored fifties showcase, just a threadbare nineties cottage.

Then it happened. In August of 1990, Saddam Hussein's forces invaded Kuwait, and not long thereafter Jim's unit was called to active duty in the Persian Gulf. Denise was left with the half-finished house projects, the bills, just enough income to avoid foreclosure or starvation, and a lonely life in San Diego. Another young man, not the military type at all but a bearded artist from Old Town, came into Denise's life. Jim got a "Dear John" letter in Saudi Arabia in January 1991, and by the following month the house was put on the market.

Something else had happened, not as devastating as the Persian Gulf conflict to be sure, but insidiously damaging nonetheless. The San Diego real estate market went soft; some said it nearly collapsed. The city enjoyed feverish, wild, unrestrained growth all through the 1980s, becoming the nation's sixth largest metropolis in the 1990 census. The general expectation was for real estate to continue to soar in value at an inflation rate of 20 percent a year. But, just as in every other city in California and most parts of the United States, San Diego real estate slowed down dramatically after 1990. New construction declined sharply, and sales of existing homes plummeted.

Denise invited a number of real estate agents to assess the value of the home, but the highest price she was quoted was $104,000. She and Jim still owed $84,000 on the original no-qualifying FHA mortgage, plus almost $10,000 on the home improvement loan, so they had a total of $94,000 debt on the property. By selling for $104,000, they'd have a margin of only $10,000, out of which the agent's commission (6 percent) would take $6,240 and the closing costs most of the rest. Even after three years in the house and a certain number of improvements, Jim and Denise couldn't sell the place for any profit at all.

In fact, they couldn't find anyone willing to pay $104,000 in the depressed market of 1991, so Denise moved back to her mother's home in Pennsylvania, leaving the house empty with a realtor's lockbox on the front door and a big FOR SALE sign in the yard. Jim came home from the war to a desolate, furniture-less settlement, and opted for quarters on the Marine base.

If the Mortons's house story seems to have a sad ending, consider that it hasn't ended yet—not for the house anyway, even if the marriage is kaput. Anybody could come along—you could—and pick up their assumable mortgage at $860 a month. The sellers in this case are so desperate they'd even take a loss just to get rid of the property and its monthly burden. Their problems will lead to someone else's gain.

Personal circumstances often lead sellers to divest themselves of good property at bargain prices, and you can take advantage of these no-credit-required deals without feeling guilty! As Mike Squires, foreclosure specialist of San Diego, says, "Look, I feel sorry for these people but I didn't create their problems." Just make sure their problems aren't inherent in the physical well-being of the house. Many a divorce has stemmed from a remodeling job.

Jim and Denise's story reflects the tragedy of returning from war to a changed domestic situation, which many Persian Gulf vets have done; but the military, to its credit, really helps its people buy a home with those VA loans (often with nothing down). The privilege of government financing has helped some veterans pull themselves up from nothing to real luxury.

Consider, for example, the experience of Dick Paulson and his Vietnamese-born wife, Kim:

They BECAME the Bank

Dick and Kim met in Saigon in 1968, married in San Francisco in 1970, and wound up settling in Seaside, California, because of its proximity to Fort Ord, where Dick was stationed as a career lieutenant in the Seventh Infantry. When he retired in his early forties, he became an independent contractor, while Kim took jobs cleaning houses for the rich ladies down in Carmel. It wasn't an easy life for the Paulsons, but with hard work and careful saving they raised three children, sent them all off to college, and leveraged their little VA home in Seaside all the way up to an ocean-view stone estate in posh Pebble Beach. They needed minimal credit to get the original VA mortgage, but now they sell houses to other people with no credit required.

Along the way, they learned the best racket in real estate, which is simply being the bank and collecting the interest. They bought small houses in need of repair for little down and, in most cases, no credit consideration, worked like the dickens on weekends, holidays, and evenings, had all three kids working alongside them plastering walls, painting ceilings, and sealing roof leaks. The restored houses were rented out and then eventually sold, with the Paulsons acting as mortgage lender. It took 20 years, but they wound up living among the privileged rich and carrying "too much real estate," as Dick complained over a McDonald's Big Mac in the Seaside location two blocks from the original family home—which he tried to sell us for $1,000 down on a personal real estate contract with no credit check.

The house was on busy Noche Buena Street, a couple of blocks on the "good" side of Broadway—real estate code for "safe." It had four bedrooms, two baths, a really pleasant kitchen, big backyard with a high fence beyond which the neighbor's dogs snarled, a peek of an ocean view, and a retaining wall crumbling over into the next-door neighbor's yard. It wasn't in bad condition, quite well kept actually, but the negative aspects that can't be changed or improved were the location on a busy street and two blocks away from "Trouble," and the highly unsociable back neighbor.

Beware of these *negative unchangables*, because they can make your house difficult to resell. You can always paint, wallpaper, landscape, re-roof, add on or beautify a home, but you can't change: the location, the neighborhood, the local job availability and economy, the climate, or the religious/social attitudes of the people.

The only other problem with Dick's no-credit home was that it was occupied by an extended family of Mexican immigrants. There was never any way to tell how many people were living there, but there were a number of children, and two women in late stages of pregnancy. They were wonderful tenants who paid the $800 rent promptly every month while keeping the house spotlessly clean, and Dick figured he had to give them the courtesy of at least six months' notice to move, because it would be hard for them to find another place. That's a long time to expect a buyer to wait to get into a house, and we were uncomfortable with the idea of displacing people from their home, but Dick sold the house eventually, of course, and some lucky buyer got a great deal without needing to even look at a banker or real estate agent. Dick, for his part, seems to enjoy the old neighborhood as much or more than his new-found opulence in Pebble Beach. He's still just a reg-ular Army guy who found a hardworking, ambitious wife in Vietnam, and together they built a substan-tial life estate on the humble path of acquiring mod-est homes and fixing them up. By now, they've built up enough credit to walk out of any bank with a million. Dick eats Big Macs in Seaside so Kim won't see him violating his low-fat diet, and McDonald's is his impromptu real estate office where he meets cli-ents and negotiates home sales.

These people and stories are all from California, but the FHA and VA mortgages are available in all 50 states, and we'll look at examples of creditless transactions from other regions. The soldier from Fort Ord could just as easily have been from Fort Devens, Massachusetts, and that house in Seaside could have been in Brockton or Dorchester. You've noticed by now that the no-qualifying government mortgages tend to be located in lower middle-class communities. They are calculated to serve the aver-age working stiff, not the top-level executive, with that $124,875 limit on the price of the home. But using some of the other methods for buying without credit in this book, there's literally no limit to what you might be able to swing. The times are certainly right. It's a buyer's market, with more property for sale than there are qualified buyers, so the sellers must make accommodations if they're serious about selling.

That $69,000 house with the swimming pool out-side of Palm Springs went on the market for $103,000 in 1991. The price was determined by a committee of 18 experts from the local board of realtors. The mortgage is automatically assumable by anyone, but its balance is only $58,000, leaving a gap of $45,000 between the loan and the asking price. No buyer is likely to put $45,000 down on a purchase of $103,000, and it wouldn't be smart to do so. We advocate the lowest down payment you can find, to tie up as little cash as possible so you can afford to work on the home, improve it, and wait for the values to go up with inflationary regularity.

If the buyers have good credit, they can simply take out a new mortgage on the place. But if there's no credit available, the buyers can still get the house in one of two ways:

With a down payment of about 10 percent, they assume the no-qualifying loan and the sellers carry the balance in a second mortgage (Deed of Trust), OR

With a somewhat larger down payment, maybe 15 percent, the sellers will act as the bank and carry the whole mortgage themselves in a "wraparound" deal. (See Chapter Four, "Owner Will Carry.")

Either way, it's paradise on the cheap, and you don't need to humiliate yourself in front of a hostile loan officer. Read on for lots more ideas and stories about how to buy *and* sell without credit. Don't be afraid—you can do it!

CHAPTER THREE

Everything About
the FHA, and More

Fifteen million American homes have been covered by Federal Housing Administration (FHA)-insured mortgages since the agency was created in 1934 in response to the Great Depression. The general idea was to make housing more affordable to a greater number of people by having the federal government insure the mortgage, even though the money itself was and is loaned by commercial banks and S&Ls. The mortgages were amortized (paid off) over a longer period of time, creating lower monthly payments, and opened with a smaller than average down payment (only 3 percent of sale price). The FHA also instituted higher construction standards.

This partnership between the government and the banks hasn't cost the taxpayers, either. The initial setup costs were repaid by 1940, and since then, the FHA has turned a profit in most years. Because the homeowners make contributions into the system, the FHA has earned the United States many billions of dollars over the years.

The way it works is that the original home buyer pays a mortgage insurance premium when he or she takes out the FHA mortgage. The rates for this premium have fluctuated over the years, but it's a small percentage of the value of the house. The money collected by FHA is kept in an insurance fund, which covers the costs of paying off mortgages when the owners go into default.

"The FHA is about the only federal government agency which has traditionally operated in the black," says Frank Baranov, manager of the FHA branch office in San Diego. "The percentage of defaults on FHA mortgages is negligible, less than one half of one percent in San Diego, but it's different in other cities."

Although the program lost money in 1990, paying off real estate loans gone sour, it's still solvent and expected to remain so, Baranov claims. As the rate of default shifts upward, the agency can charge a higher insurance premium to keep its fund at a safe level.

The FHA doesn't keep records on exactly how many of those 15 million mortgages have been assumed by new buyers, but certainly a huge number have been, some of them many times. The FHA itself doesn't even learn of the assumption, which is handled by the bank, unless the new owner falls into default on the loan.

It strikes us as poetically fitting that the same program invented to relieve the huge economic woes of the Depression should now be helping people buy a home in the age of tight credit in the 1990s recession, or whatever history will finally label this slump we're in.

And even though home foreclosures and personal bankruptcy are way up in today's economy, there is no danger or likelihood of the FHA going under as long as the U.S. government is in business. It is the cornerstone of affordable house ownership in the nation. In 1986, the FHA insured 750,000 mortgages, for a 20 percent share of the national mortgage market.

It's true that in the 1970s and 1980s, FHA activity

declined as the housing market heated up and prices soared. And remember that today's FHA standards for new mortgages definitely require the buyer to qualify for credit. But those millions of older FHA mortgages in all states of the Union continue to help the lower- and middle-income buyer with inadequate credit. Few government agencies have been as successful and humanely beneficial as our good old FHA. A January 1986 *Real Estate Finance Today* survey showed the majority of FHA borrowers had less than $1,100 cash to their names after paying closing costs. In other words, without FHA financing, many low- or moderate-income buyers would be unable to afford a home.

Incidentally, the Reagan administration actually proposed selling the FHA to private interests. That option was raised in its 1987 fiscal year budget. With FHA reserves sitting at more than $4 billion at the time, the sale of the FHA would have brought in considerable funds to reduce the national debt and the government's involvement in business. But "such a sale would eliminate the social purpose integral to the FHA program," according to the Mortgage Bankers Association of America position paper, *The Federal Housing Administration, Past, Present, and Future.* "It would only serve to eliminate homeownership opportunities to families with no other avenue of financing available."

The sale proposal never came to pass. It would have been just one more case of the rich getting richer, the poor poorer. It's fairly certain that no private bank or mortgage lender would let a person without credit assume an existing mortgage. We could become a nation of renters, with a small elite of landlords collecting money from a large underclass of tenants, even more than is now the case.

In the first few years of the 1990s, the FHA has

been financially beleaguered, but hardly bankrupt. The problem lost $1.3 billion during fiscal 1990, according to Housing and Urban Development (HUD) secretary Jack Kemp's address to Congress in October 1991. That loss was attributed to two funds that are not designed to be self-supporting and that absorb losses in the multifamily-dwelling insurance program. The FHA is simply reflecting hard times in the real estate lending business. Those hard times can actually make it easier for you to buy a home without credit.

A Word About Interest Rates

FHA assumable no-qualifying mortgages are transferred to the buyer at the same interest rate the seller has been paying. That can produce a tremendous advantage to you if the original mortgage was written in an era of low interest rates, and the rate on the house is fixed.

Most FHA mortgages do have a fixed rate, but some of the newer ones have an adjustable rate mortgage (ARM). If you buy a house with an adjustable rate, you'll pay the rate the seller is currently paying, but with no guarantee that it will stay the same. Adjustable rates were quite low in the early 1990s, but the hazard of such a rate is that it can skyrocket when inflation hits. Many a homeowner has been dismayed, or even forced out of the home, when the monthly payment suddenly goes way up. The rate adjustment is tied to a financial index, such as the U.S. Securities Treasury Index.

In general, we favor a fixed interest rate if it's under 10 percent, but we're not prepared to say that the adjustable rate is absolutely unacceptable. If you're without credit, you have to take the best assumable mortgage you can find, and an adjustable rate might let you get started in home ownership at a more affordable price.

The FHA is administered by HUD and is one of the most successful federal programs in our history. It is solidly behind the American homeowner despite an upturn in delinquencies and foreclosures in recent years, and notwithstanding recent reforms that have tightened its standards considerably. There has been no suggestion of eliminating the older assumable mortgages.

HUD will send you, free of charge, an upbeat little booklet called *A Home of Your Own, Helpful Advice from HUD on Choosing, Buying, and Enjoying a Home*. It doesn't contain any particular advice on buying without credit, but it makes a lot of good, basic points about home buying in general. Write to U.S. Government Publications, Pueblo, Colorado, and ask for pamphlet HUD-1290-SFPD(1).

Remember, there are still millions of those assumable no-qualifying FHA mortgages out there, but you have to ask for them by name. It's astonishing to us that many real estate agents don't even know these basic facts. Tell the agent, up front and in no uncertain terms, that you are looking for a home with an FHA assumable no-qualifying mortgage, and if the agent doesn't know what that means, show them this book.

CHAPTER FOUR

Owner Will Carry

Suppose you just can't find a house for sale with one of those magical FHA no-qualifying mortgages? Or you find one, but the mortgage balance is far below the asking price, and of course you don't have the credit to qualify for a new mortgage?

Don't despair! As wonderful as those FHA assumable mortgages are, they are **not** the most popular or conventional way that people without credit can buy a home. Without a doubt, the usual way that people buy without needing to have bank or lender approval is through seller financing. The sellers, like our friends the Paulsons in Chapter Two, act as the bank. Instead of paying a bank or mortgage company, you make out your monthly check to the previous owners of the house.

With such an arrangement, you legally and absolutely own the house (and have every right to resell it) just as if you had purchased it through a bank. But the only "bank" you need to convince to trust you is the seller(s).

Search through the real estate classified section of your local newspaper for terms like "owner will carry," "seller financing possible," "owner MAY carry," "OWC," or "OWC 2nd." These are tipoffs that the sellers have already formed a favorable impression of carrying the financing themselves.

Although there are many excellent reasons why

they should, not every seller is willing to do so. In the first place, the seller who carries the financing stands to make much more money from the sale of the house. Most mortgage payments are more than 90 percent interest, less than 10 percent principal, in the early years especially. If you're paying $1,000 a month to the previous owner of the house, chances are that more than $900 of it is interest charges. You're only gaining less than $100 on the sum you owe, the principal balance.

In short, over a typical 20- to 30-year mortgage period, you will actually pay two to three times or more the sale price of the house. If the seller carries the loan for that long, he or she is likely to get triple the price for the house!

That is the way mortgages are "amortized," or paid off. The system works in favor of the bank, or in these cases, the seller who is acting as the bank. For example, let's say you buy a $60,000 house with owner financing, put up a $10,000 down payment, and pay the seller a mortgage of $50,000 over 20 years at an interest rate of $9\frac{1}{2}$ percent. Your monthly payment works out to be $466.07. (You can get a complete set of mortgage amortization tables from your local real estate broker, banker, library, or bookseller.)

When you make the first payment of $466.07, you do not reduce the amount you owe on the house by very much. In fact, less than a dollar goes against the principal amount owed, whereas $465 of the $466 is interest paid. The $50,000 owed is still $49,999 and change.

With every month that passes, the proportion of interest goes down and principal goes up. Halfway through the 20 years, your $466 is evenly divided, half to interest and half to principal.

If you make this same payment every month for

the full 20 years, you will have paid $111,856.80 on that $50,000 mortgage. The seller winds up collecting $121,856.80, more than double the price of the house, over time.

If the same $60,000 house, with the same down payment, stretches a $50,000 mortgage over a 30-year term, the monthly payment goes down to $420.43, but the final amount paid for the house soars to $161,354.80.

The property itself is the security for the loan, so if you fail to make your payments, the seller always has the option to foreclose and take the house back, in which case you'd lose every dime you put into it. But the average seller doesn't want to think about such a possibility any more than you, the buyer, would. The seller just wants to find buyers who are definitely and positively going to come up with the payment, so he or she can be free of worry.

What kind of people will agree to finance the sale of their house? You'd be surprised. They don't have to be rich, but they have to be comfortable enough that they don't need to cash out of their house on selling it. Some owners simply must cash out because they need the money to purchase another home or for some other urgent reason. But a lot of sellers already have another place to move, and for tax reasons in addition to the greater income, they prefer to carry the mortgage.

• Older people about to retire or move into a nursing home, convenient apartment, or an adult child's home, are excellent candidates for seller financing. If the children have grown and moved out, and/or a spouse has died, an elderly seller may want to be rid of the work and expense of maintaining a big home. For such a person, seller financing provides a stable monthly check, a comfortable retirement income. If he or she dies before the mortgage is paid off, you continue making your payments to the heirs or the estate.

• Sellers trapped in a slow (or dead) real estate market may consider financing the sale themselves, because it makes their home much easier to sell. If you look for a house that's been on the market for at least six months without a sale, you're more likely to find a seller who'll at least consider an offer to finance the deal. If you can come up with a decent down payment (sometimes not even that), the seller may prefer to carry the financing and get a monthly check rather than have the house sit there unsold, producing nothing but heartache.

• Property in bad condition is a prime candidate for "owner will carry." Banks and lending institutions have certain standards for the house as well as the purchaser, and often if the house has a particular defect (like a cracked-slab foundation, or no foundation at all, an inadequate sized lot that prohibits additions, a zoning problem, or an illegal mother-in-law apartment that must be torn down), no bank will issue a mortgage on it—no matter how good the buyer's credit may be. In such cases, and there are many, the seller has no choice but to carry the loan, unless he or she can find a buyer willing to pay all cash up front.

Be careful! If you get into an owner-financed deal on a house that no bank will touch, you're going to have the same problem yourself when you or your heirs try to sell the house someday. (And let's face it, sooner or later the house will probably be sold again. Very few people keep a house from generation to generation.)

Therefore, consider these points:

1. Make sure whatever defect the house has is something you can comfortably live with or, better yet, something you can fix. On the West Coast and in the Sunbelt states, some houses lack foundations, but the weather is mild, so you don't really need a basement. The bank may disapprove, but you may not even care. You can always jack up a house and put a foundation under it, but that's complicated and costly. Other defects are much simpler and cheaper to fix.

2. If you buy a house that's got something wrong with it, which prohibits a bank mortgage, you **don't** want a "due-on-sale" clause in your mortgage. That kind of clause obligates you to cash out the seller in the event you resell the house again, and that'll be almost impossible if the place can't qualify for a conventional loan. You want the right to sell the house to still another buyer, and finance it yourself. Some houses are carried from owner to owner like that through three or even four mortgages.

• Sellers who have already moved (because of job transfer or other personal reasons) are good candidates to carry the financing. If the house is empty and the owner is still paying his own mortgage plus taxes and insurance, as well as the expenses on the new home, he or she may be financially distressed and happy to have someone else—anyone else—paying for the old property.

• Owners who have already paid off their mortgages are in great shape to finance your purchase. They don't even have to make a payment themselves and can pocket every cent of your payment. But even those who are still paying off their own mortgages can finance yours in a "wraparound" mortgage, as long as they don't have one of those dreadful "due-on-sale" clauses on their own mortgage.

A "wraparound" mortgage is one in which the buyer pays the seller a monthly mortgage payment, while the seller continues to pay an existing earlier mortgage. Legally, it's sometimes called an "overriding or all-inclusive trust deed."

If the seller's own mortgage has a "due-on-sale" clause, it must be cashed out when the house is sold. Therefore, the seller could not finance a wraparound. Many sellers can do it, however, and it's a great opportunity for the buyer without credit.

• Sometimes a seller who is reluctant to carry a mortgage may be willing to do so if you set a reasonable time limitation followed by a "balloon payment." In other words, the seller agrees to finance you for five years, for example, at the end of which time you agree to find new financing and cash the seller out for whatever amount is still owed on the house. The assumption here is that after five years, the property will be worth far more than when you bought it, and you'll be able to find new financing more easily. A big balloon payment is always a risk, but it's a very common practice in private real estate contracts, and it usually works fine. (But you may lose sleep as that balloon approaches . . .)

• "Location is everything," according to the old real estate saying. A house that's in a great location, where most people would love to live, is not as likely to be available without credit or through seller financing. (Although there are exceptions to this and every rule.) Generally, if the location of the house is somewhat less than perfect, you've got a better chance. But please don't go out and buy a house situated next door to the county dump simply because it's cheap and offers seller financing. Choose a location with enough natural appeal that you'll be able to sell the house to someone else someday.

• Remember that houses for *rent* and houses that don't specifically offer owner financing may still be available without credit through "owner-will-carry" techniques. It's simply up to you to convince the landlord/owner to sell it to you on that basis. Here's where it pays to get creative. But if you don't feel you can be creative enough to pull it off, you can always seek out a real estate agent who will make the offer for you, called a "buyer's agent." Seller financing deals often don't require an agent, however. Any seller who is willing to carry the mortgage is probably sophisticated enough to write up the deal without needing an agent's services and without having to pay that agent's commission. If a sales agent brings you to the home and writes up the purchase, the seller will have to pay that person's commission even if he carries the financing, so some sellers will flatly refuse to deal with agents. If you see the phrase "principals only" or "for sale by owner" in an ad, it means just that.

We are not opposed to agents. To the contrary, we believe that in *most* cases it is preferable to use one—yes, even with owner financing. Many people just don't know how to conduct a legal, binding agreement, and the intricacies of the real estate contract may be too daunting. A good, reputable agent also acts as a third-party buffer between seller and buyer, and can negotiate the terms back and forth with less emotional involvement than the principal players. Not to knock young people, but when we're house-hunting, we look for an experienced agent who's handled many no-credit deals in the past.

(See the Real Estate Contract form at the end of this chapter. You can use this form word for word for your purchase or get a similar document from any well-stocked stationery store.)

How to Talk the Seller Into Being the Bank

If the house is being advertised with "owner will carry" terms, you just have to convince the seller that you're capable of meeting his or her price and terms. But if you have to convince the seller to carry the financing, you will need to be more creative and persuasive. Here's some good and time-tested advice:

• **Make an offer in writing.** Oral or spoken agreements have no worth at all in real estate. Only a formal offer in writing can initiate a sale, and that written offer is what the seller is waiting to see. Of course, you can talk about the house and your offer all you want, but unless you get it on paper, it's not an offer.

• **Show the seller how much he or she is going to profit from carrying the financing.** A lot of people don't realize how much more they could get for their home by carrying the mortgage. The Smiths are selling their $75,000 home and still owe $25,000 on it, for example, so they figure they're going to get about $50,000 out of the sale. If, instead, you give them $10,000 down and pay them about $700 a month at 9 or 10 percent interest, it's possible they could wind up receiving $150,000 or $200,000 for their $75,000 home. If you can demonstrate to a seller exactly how much more money he'll get by "being the bank," he may go for it. Use standard mortgage amortization interest tables, which you can get from your bank, savings and loan, or local real estate broker.

Some Typical Mortgage Tables

Complete mortgage tables could literally take up hundreds of pages here, because they vary widely based on three factors:

- The interest rate
- The length or "term" of the loan
- The amount of the principal, or the amount owed

In the 1980s, we saw interest rates inflated up into the high teens; 14 to 17 percent was not uncommon. A decade later, in the practical 1990s, the opposite trend has taken place. Fixed rates are sometimes as low as 8 percent, and adjustable rates lower than that. There's simply no way to guarantee here what interest rates are going to do in the future, because they depend on the health of the economy in general.

For the sake of example, however, let's look at mortgage amortization tables ranging between 7 and 10 percent, for amounts ranging from $50,000 to $100,000, over a period ranging from 10 to 30 years. Note how much difference even a quarter of a percentage point makes.

MONTHLY MORTGAGE PAYMENT
AT 7½% INTEREST

TERM	10 YEARS	20 YEARS	30 YEARS
AMOUNT of mortgage:			
$ 50,000	$ 593.50	$402.80	$349.61
60,000	712.21	483.35	419.53
70,000	830.91	563.91	489.45
80,000	949.61	644.47	559.37
90,000	1,068.31	725.03	629.29
100,000	1,187.01	805.59	699.21

MONTHLY MORTGAGE PAYMENT
AT 7¾% INTEREST

TERM	10 YEARS	20 YEARS	30 YEARS
AMOUNT of mortgage:			
$ 50,000	$ 600.05	$410.47	$358.20
60,000	720.06	492.56	429.84
70,000	840.07	574.66	501.48
80,000	960.08	656.75	573.13
90,000	1,080.09	738.85	644.77
100,000	1,200.10	820.94	716.41

MONTHLY MORTGAGE PAYMENT
AT 8% INTEREST

TERM	10 YEARS	20 YEARS	30 YEARS
AMOUNT of mortgage:			
$ 50,000	$ 606.63	$418.22	$366.88
60,000	727.96	501.86	440.25
70,000	849.29	585.50	513.63
80,000	970.62	669.15	587.01
90,000	1.091.94	752.79	660.38
100,000	1,213.27	836.44	733.76

MONTHLY MORTGAGE PAYMENT
AT 8¼% INTEREST

TERM	10 YEARS	20 YEARS	30 YEARS
AMOUNT of mortgage:			
$ 50,000	$ 613.26	$426.03	$375.63
60,000	735.91	511.23	450.75
70,000	858.56	596.44	525.88
80,000	981.22	681.65	601.01
90,000	1,103.87	766.85	676.13
100,000	1,226.52	852.06	751.26

MONTHLY MORTGAGE PAYMENT
AT 8½% INTEREST

TERM	10 YEARS	20 YEARS	30 YEARS
AMOUNT of mortgage:			
$ 50,000	$ 619.93	$433.91	$384.45
60,000	743.91	520.69	461.34
70,000	867.90	607.47	538.23
80,000	991.88	694.26	615.13
90,000	1,115.87	781.04	692.02
100,000	1,239.85	867.82	768.91

Analyzing these figures, you'll find that if you are carrying a mortgage balance of $100,000, your monthly payment could be anywhere between $665 and $1,321, which is a huge difference, depending on the interest rate and how long the mortgage term is. And remember, that's only between 7 and 10 percent. If the interest were only 6 percent or as high as 11 percent, the difference would be even more staggering.

Consider this, too: at 9 percent amortized over 10 years, you would pay a total of *$152,011.20* on a $100,000 mortgage. On the same mortgage amount, except at 10 percent and amortized over 30 years, you would pay a total of *$315,928.80*, more than twice as much.

If you can show the seller figures like this, solid indications of how much profit there is in extending seller financing, you just might convince someone to be your bank.

A final note: Although standard tables are available at your bank, real estate office, library, or bookstore, in today's computerized world they are somewhat cumbersome. Any banker or real estate agent with a computer can tell you in an instant exactly what your mortgage payment would be, just by plugging into the computer the amount, the term, and the interest rate. A book of standard, printed tables may be useful to you, however, in writing up your offer to the seller.

• **Convince the seller that you're going to make the payments on time.** This gets tricky, of course, since you have inadequate credit, or perhaps none at all. But if you can't make the payments on time, you shouldn't be buying the house. If there's anyone in your household who has a steady job, inform the seller of this stable employment and tell him how much the salary is. Offer the employer's name and phone number as a reference.

If you're self-employed, it might help to present the seller with photocopies of your last three years' income tax returns. (Unless of course they prove beyond a doubt that you're losing money in your business.)

If you're now paying rent and are not behind in your payments, by all means give the seller your landlord's name and phone number as a reference. This can be the ultimate convincing tactic. If you're trying to take on a $700 mortgage payment and you've been paying $600 rent in a timely fashion every month, the seller has every reason to believe you can swing it. On the other hand, if your rent is only $300 and you're trying to move up to a $1,000 mortgage obligation, you may need to do a bit more convincing.

Do you have assets other than income or job, something that could literally be cashed in if the need arose? Don't hesitate to make a list of these things and present it to the seller as part of your net worth. A lot of folks without good credit nonetheless own a fine automobile, a valuable collection of baseball cards (some are priceless), family heirlooms, jewelry, electronics equipment, you name it.

• **Offer some kind of down payment, no matter how modest.**   You can still buy property for "nothing down" in some circumstances, but the average seller will not be interested. The owner has probably put a great deal of money and work into the house over a long period, and the idea of getting nothing up front for selling it will be deeply insulting. It's an emotional as well as financial transaction when you're dealing directly with the seller.

Banks try to insist on a down payment as high as 20 percent of the sale price, and it would be great if you could come up with 10 percent down in a seller-financed deal, but these guidelines are general and completely open to negotiation. In today's tough market, with a lot of people out of work and having credit difficulties, even 5 percent down may be too much.

But offer something—not nothing—down. Dick Paulson in Chapter Two was willing to take $1,000 down on a house worth more than $100,000. Why? "Because the thousand bucks tells me you're serious," he said. "If you get in there with nothing down, it's just like paying rent. You haven't made any commitment at all. Then if you stop making payments, it could take me months to evict you and I've got nothing for my trouble, and you could even trash the house." A mere thousand made that much difference to him.

• **Find a house for rent and offer the landlord more than the rent if he'll sell it with owner financing.**   Throw in a down payment, too. If the asking price for the rent is $600 a month, go to the landlord and say, "I'll pay you $750 a month for that house and $x,000 down if you'll sell it to me on a private real estate contract with owner financing." Right away, he's getting a few thousand dollars up front and getting a much higher monthly payment for the property. If the landlord is financially strapped or even just a little greedy, he or she may accept your offer.

The Private Real Estate Contract

A private real estate contract between buyer and seller is just like a bank-mortgaged purchase agreement in that it is a legal document stating *all* the particulars of the sale. You may want to have an attorney check the document before you sign. Just as in most deals, you'll be expected to produce a check for "earnest money," usually a small amount used to open an escrow account. How small is small? That depends on the cost of the house. In some cases, $500 to $1,000 will be enough. The only danger is that if you change your mind and back out of the deal, the earnest money may not be refundable. The seller may get to keep it in exchange for releasing the buyer from the sale. Always make your earnest money check out to the real estate agency or the escrow company, *not* directly to the sellers.

The contract contains the full names of all sellers and buyers, a legal description of the property (available from your county recorder's office—the street address of the house is usually not sufficient to constitute a legal description), the price of the property and all the terms (including the amount of down payment, the amount of monthly payment, the interest rate of the loan, the number of years the mortgage is to run, the balloon payment if any, the agent's commission if any), a date of purchase, and projected date of closing.

Many other details can be added to the contract. If the house has fixtures or personal property that are included in the sale, they should be mentioned specifically. You don't want an argument later when you discover the sellers have removed the blinds, curtains, chandelier, or refrigerator. It's better to spell everything out in the most specific terms: include a list of all the things that will remain with the property. In some states, the sellers are also required to sign a list of "disclosures," essentially guaranteeing that everything in the house is in working order, or else specifically naming problems or needed repairs. It is illegal for someone to hide defects in the house they sell you, but beware—to get legal recourse later, you'd have to prove that the seller knew of the defect and deliberately lied about it. Be sure to get the disclosures in writing at the outset.

If the seller insists on a clause stating that the house is being sold in "as-is condition," be especially wary. "As-is" almost always means there's some problem(s) that the seller doesn't want to be responsible for in the future.

The seller must promise in writing to deliver a valid, legal, and clear title to the property. This assures you that there isn't some other person or institution with a claim to the deed. In most cases, it's wise to take out a title insurance policy, which for a modest fee will cover you in case your title is "clouded" by previous claimants.

Insurance and taxes figure into this private contract, too. Always insist that the seller maintain insurance on the house at least equal to the sale price up to the day of closing, and always make arrangements for your new insurance policy to begin at the same time. The house should never be left uninsured for a moment. What if it burns down while you're at the escrow office signing papers?

Of course, the contract must be dated and properly signed by both sellers and buyers. Sometimes, the escrow company or agent will need your signatures verified by a notary, especially if you can't be there in person for the "closing" ceremonies. We recommend that you do attend in person, just for the thrill of being handed the deed to the ranch. But never try to make last-minute changes in the deal just as you're about to close; you could create problems that kill the sale or postpone it indefinitely. Get your private real estate contract in good order and you shouldn't need to amend anything later.

THE PRIVATE REAL ESTATE CONTRACT

(You can copy this contract word for word, typing it out on white paper, or get a standard form at a stationery store. In any case, read it to familiarize yourself with the contract and its terms.)

Real Estate Purchase Contract and Receipt for Deposit
Name of city and state, Date , *199-*

Received from   (hereinafter called
"Buyer") the sum of   dollars ($)
evidenced by cash ( ), cashier's check ( ), personal
check ( ), or   ( ), payable to   ,
to be held uncashed until acceptance of this offer, as deposit on the account of the total purchase price of
dollars ($) for the purchase of that certain real
property and all improvements located thereon situated
in County, state of   , and described as follows:

1. Buyer will deposit in escrow with   *(name of escrow holder)*   the total purchase price as follows:
A. The above deposit shall be delivered by Broker ( )
Seller ( ) to the escrow holder promptly upon Seller's
acceptance hereof for the account of the Buyer.
B. The total cash down payment to be deposited with
escrow, including the above amount, is: dollars
($)
C. Seller's Purchase Money Carryback. The balance of
the purchase price is to be evidenced by a Note secured
by a Trust Deed on the property in the amount of
dollars ($) executed by the Buyer in favor of
the Seller, including interest at   percent (%) per an-
num, to accrue from close of escrow. Principal and interest payable monthly in installments of
dollars ($) or more, beginning on the first day
of each month after the close of escrow, all due and
payable   years from close of escrow. A late
charge of   dollars ($) shall be
due on any payment tendered more than ten (10) days late.
This is an all-inclusive Note secured by a Deed of Trust
for a total purchase price of   dollars
($).

2. Upon mutual execution of this contract, the parties
shall execute escrow instructions to the escrow holder in
accordance with the terms and provisions hereof, which
shall constitute joint instructions to the escrow holder.
The parties shall execute additional instructions re-
quested by the escrow holder not inconsistent with the
provisions hereof. Said escrow shall provide for a closing
on or before

3. As soon as reasonably possible after opening of escrow, Seller shall provide the Buyer a Preliminary Title Report on the subject property, together with full copies of all exceptions set forth therein, including but not limited to covenants, conditions, restrictions, reservations, easements, rights and rights of way, liens and other matters of record. Buyer shall have ( ) days after receipt of said Preliminary Title Report within which to notify the Seller and the escrow holder, in writing, of Buyer's disapproval of any exceptions shown in said Title Report. Seller shall have until the date of closing of escrow to attempt to eliminate any disapproved exceptions from the policy of Title Insurance to be issued in favor of Buyer and, if not eliminated, then the escrow shall be cancelled unless Buyer elects to waive his prior disapproval. Failure of Buyer to disapprove any exceptions within the aforementioned time limit shall constitute approval of said Preliminary Title Report. The policy of Title Insurance shall be issued by (*title insurance company*) with a liability limited to the total purchase price and shall be paid for by Seller.

4. Seller shall furnish a structural pest control report showing accessible areas of buildings upon the property to be free of infestation caused by wood-destroying insects, fungi, or dry rot. Seller shall pay for any corrective work required.

5. Title shall vest as follows: *name of title holder(s)*

6. Buyer and Seller agree that fixtures and fittings attached to the property, including but not limited to window shades, curtains, blinds, built-in and attached appliances, light fixtures, plumbing fixtures, carpeting, air conditioners, trees, shrubs, mailbox and other similar items, if applicable, are included, but no personal property except as specified below:

7. If Buyer fails to complete said purchase as herein provided by reason of any default of Buyer, Seller shall be released from any obligation to sell the property to Buyer and may proceed against Buyer upon any claim or

remedy in law. By placing their initials here, however, Buyer ( ) and Seller ( ) agree that Seller shall retain the deposit as his liquidated damages.

8. Possession shall be delivered to Buyer on close of escrow.

9. Real property taxes and premiums on insurance on the forementioned property shall be prorated between Seller and Buyer as of the date of closing of escrow. Buyer and Seller agree to each pay one half ($\frac{1}{2}$) of escrow fees.

10. If the property is destroyed or materially damaged between the date of this contract and the date of closing of escrow, Buyer shall have the option to declare in writing that this contract is null and void, and under such circumstances Seller shall waive any right to retain Buyer's deposit.

11. This constitutes a legal and binding offer to purchase the above described property. Unless acceptance is signed by Seller and delivered to Buyer in person or by mail to the address below, with   days from the date hereof, this offer shall be revoked and the deposit returned to Buyer. Buyer acknowledges receipt of a copy hereof.

SIGNED:

Broker: _____   Buyer: _____
Address: _____   Address: _____
_____   _____
Phone: _____   Phone: _____

ACCEPTANCE

The undersigned Seller accepts and agrees to sell the above described property on the above terms and conditions. Seller has employed   *name of broker*   and

agrees to pay a commission for services rendered in the amount of
dollars ($) upon the closing of escrow and recording of deed or other evidence of title, OR if the completion of the sale is prevented by default of Seller, upon Seller's default. The undersigned Seller acknowledges receipt of a copy of this contract and authorizes Broker to deliver a signed copy to Buyer.

Seller: _____   Broker: _____
Date: _____   Date: _____
Address: _____   Address: _____
_____   _____
Phone: _____   Phone: _____

Notes on This Real Estate Contract

This is a highly simplified version of the contract, based on a number of actual ones that we've signed in the past. Every real estate contract should include these clauses, but some will add many more.

People sometimes think there's a formal, set, "correct" way to do this, and in fact you should have the legal protection of at least these: a solid title insurance policy, proper vesting of title, the security of a bonded escrow holder.

You can buy a title insurance policy from any reputable title insurance company. In most towns, an escrow company officer or real estate broker will be glad to recommend a local title insurance company. Your best safety is in the longevity and reputation of that company. Basically, title insurance companies take the risk of a bad or flawed title away from you and onto their own shoulders. Typically, they research the ownership of the house for as many years in the past as they can find records. Those records of past transfers of title can make for some very entertaining reading on winter nights, while you are enjoying the warmth of your new home!

"Vesting" of title refers to the name or names in which the deed is to be recorded. The verb "to vest" means simply "to bestow upon." The former owner "vests" the title on you, the new owner. Be sure that title is vested to your formal, proper name(s). Don't have title vested to "Don Jones" if your name is Donald Anthony Jones III. As far-fetched as it might sound, there could be some other "Don Jones" somewhere who could contest your title.

The real estate agent's commission is also completely open to negotiation. If an agent tells you the "standard" commission is 6 percent or whatever, don't believe it. There is no such thing as a standard commission, but there is a typical rate in any given area. Let your agent make an honest living. But especially with owner financing, you can sweeten the deal for the seller by operating without an agent or lowering the commission rate offered.

Clause 9 involves taxes, and the "proration" of taxes between buyer and seller. Proration simply means that buyer and seller each will pay their share of the tax based on the day that the ownership transfers.

Taxes are an important issue, of course. In many cases, the mortgage payment will include both the taxes and insurance in monthly installments, so you make only one payment, and you're covered. But in other instances, you'll have to pay your local government a real estate tax that is levied once or twice a year. If you're buying a house, be sure to find out how much the taxes are and how they are paid.

There is no standard real estate tax rate; it varies from place to place. The state of New Hampshire, which has no sales or income tax, compensates somewhat with relatively high property taxes. In California, taxes were actually rolled back in the 1980s due to a voters' initiative.

The tax you pay on your home will be determined by the local tax rate and the government's assessed value of your property. These assessments are frequently lower than the fair market value, especially if one owner has held the property for a long time.

Always make sure that your tax is paid, because the government can eventually take the property away from you and sell it at auction to pay off back taxes due.

Owners Who Carried, and How It All Worked Out

A bunch of us, good friends, got together in 1968 and bought a 100-acre farm in Vermont from an elderly widow who had spent most of her life on the property, saw her children grow and move out, and her husband die there. She just wanted a reliable monthly income to finance her retirement nest in an "all electric apartment" in the nearby town of Brattleboro. The farm had only wood heat and no indoor toilet, was located on a steep dirt road, often snowed in during winter, and generally lacked the comforts and proximity to services that most elderly people need.

We just wanted a retreat from urban stress, a place in the country where artists and writers could gather and stay to work in peace, recharge our batteries.

Rosie Franklin was nobody's fool. She realized that if she sold the property for cash, she'd have an enormous tax liability and lose a big part of her money. She also knew that by carrying the mortgage, she would eventually get twice the price for the house and acreage. But since she was in her early seventies and didn't expect to live another 20 years, she insisted on a 10-year mortgage, at 10 percent interest. We bought the place for $25,000, with $5,000 down payment and a mortgage of $227.10 a month. That was real money in 1968. Rosie added a provision that although we were buying her farm and would own it, she retained the lifetime right to pick peaches from her orchard once a week during harvest time. This was a delightful touch, and we didn't mind sharing the peaches with her in the least.

On the first day of every month, one of us went into town and gave Rosie her $227.10—sometimes in cash, for which she gave us a handwritten receipt— and then we checked off another payment on our mortgage balance printout, which was posted on the kitchen wall. There were occasions when we couldn't come up with the entire $227.10 at once, so we brought Rosie whatever amount we had scraped up and finished the payment later in the month. We never actually got a full month behind in the payments, and Rosie was always sympathetic and understanding when we were hard up, but she literally needed our mortgage payment to pay her own rent, groceries, and doctor bills, and we felt responsible. She also held the farm itself as collateral for her loan, so if we'd failed to pay she could have exercised her right to take the property back.

Exactly ten years later, we made the final payment to Rosie's daughter, because Rosie herself had gone to her Heavenly reward just before the mortgage expired. We burned the mortgage and had a hell of a great party. The farm is still in our hands more than

20 years later, having been incorporated as an artist's foundation in the meantime.

In the meantime, too, it's gone from being worth $25,000 to hundreds of thousands. We were lucky in that we bought property in Vermont while the state was economically depressed and before the great surge of back-to-the-land urban refugees began arriving in the seventies. Shortly thereafter, skiers started coming in much greater numbers, tony classical music festivals sprang up, then with the birth of the Yuppies it became chic for people in New York and Boston to own a second home ("chalet," no less) in Vermont.

When we bought the farm, it had no full-time, year-round neighbors closer than two miles away. We found out the place was vacant and for sale because a college friend from Boston had a weekend getaway cabin down the road apiece. It was never advertised and nobody in the small town where it was located could afford to buy it. Rosie didn't like her late husband's relatives anyway, and was determined not to let the property fall into their hands. We just stumbled onto this opportunity.

There was no real estate agent, no bank, not even an escrow company involved in the purchase. A trusted attorney and judge in town, one Judge Chapman, represented both seller and buyers, handled the escrow, and filed the deed with the county. The farm people have staged a number of Shakespearean plays and summer organ concerts in a nearby barn, and a veritable five-foot shelf of published books has been written at the farm, which has been variously called Packer Corners Farm, Total Loss Farm, or the Monteverdi Artists Collaborative.

But, you say, nowadays you couldn't buy an old farm from a widow without credit, agent, bank, or escrow company. Or could you? Of course you can.

This case is a perfect example of picking up unwanted rural property, and in fact some rural areas of the United States are severely depressed in the 1990s. All you need to find is an older house and a desperate seller somewhere way out in the country where there are few jobs and a sagging local economy.

In fact, this kind of living has become more practical with the advent of telecommuting, fax machines, home computers, sophisticated telephone lines, and such. If your rural home is within even a long commuting distance to your job, and you can work at home some days of the week or send in your work via modem or fax, it could be easier than ever to live in the country and enjoy the peace of nature. We know executives from Los Angeles who are willing to drive three hours each way to live in Big Bear up in the mountains, or Idyllwild in the desert, in exchange for much cheaper homes with more living space, better conditions for their children to grow up in, less crime, and cleaner air. If you work in Boston, for example, you might be able to live on some pretty country road in New Hampshire and pay a tenth as much for a house. The economy in some parts of New England is in terrible shape in the 1990s, and there are credit-free deals out there.

But owner financing is certainly not limited to rural backwaters. Plenty of urban property is available also, especially if the city in question has experienced massive layoffs or if there is some kind of "flight" going on. Seattle, Washington, was virtually a ghost town in the 1970s, after Boeing Aircraft laid off thousands of workers. Every neighborhood had empty houses with assumable FHA mortgages, homes that had been abandoned by people who went elsewhere looking for jobs. "Will the last person to leave Seattle please turn off the lights," said a huge downtown billboard.

Married with children at the time, author Ray Mungo bought a fabulous large Victorian home with dazzling view of Lake Union from a young dentist and his wife who were moving out to a new suburb for more opportunity than Seattle could offer. We paid $20,000 for the house, with the dentist carrying the mortgage himself since the banks had stopped issuing mortgages and we didn't have enough credit. A few years later, and after a divorce, we sold the place for $48,000, cashing out the dentist and splitting the profits 50/50. The Seattle economy had picked up some, and we'd extensively remodeled and improved the property.

Detroit and environs, Houston, Phoenix, Denver, Pittsburgh, the industrial Northeast and coal belt have all had economic reversals in recent years, while the population has been streaming into Florida and California. If you really want to find a great owner-will-carry deal, look in areas where other people have been leaving; try to find an area that has innate value and natural resources, a place that will swing back into prosperity.

Don't rely solely on the daily newspaper classifieds, although they are invaluable—especially those that specify "owner will carry." Some people advertise in smaller, weekly or monthly free newspapers, and some just post a sign in the front yard. Drive around to the neighborhoods that interest you on Sunday afternoons. Talk to your friends or co-workers and let them know you're looking for a house the seller will finance. It's surprising how many deals are made between private parties on property that's never been advertised.

Now More Than Ever, Owner May Carry

The times are certainly right for owner financing. The real estate business is in a nationwide slump in the early nineties. The last time it was this slow, seller financing also took a huge leap in popularity. We're talking about the period from 1981 to 1983, when inflation was rampant and mortgage interest rates went sky-high. A lot of people couldn't countenance paying up to 14 percent interest on a mortgage, so the sellers were forced to carry some paper if they wanted a sale.

This bit of history shows us that no-credit transactions are just as useful, possible, and popular no matter what state the economy might be in. Real estate values tend to go in cycles, and surely the slump of the early 1990s will be replaced by a stronger, more lucrative market when our national economy rebounds after the recession.

We've bought property without credit in both good and bad times. The swimming pool home in Morongo Valley was purchased at the peak of real estate values in 1989, just before the recession set in.

There are several reasons why you will always be able to buy without credit, even when the economy is sound and prices are high. With an FHA or VA assumable mortgage transaction, for example, the seller is interested only in getting the difference between the mortgage balance and the sale price. And some sellers will always be willing to carry the mortgage, simply because it is so much more profitable for them.

In 1978, approximately four million existing single-family homes were sold in the nation. But in 1982, when sales hit rock bottom, fewer than two million were sold. Business was cut in half. Sales went back up to the four million level in a gradual, year-by-year increase up to 1989.

In that bleak 1982 season, Dwight and Jane Marshall decided to sell their wonderful adobe home in Santa Fe, New Mexico. Their carefully planned baby turned out to be twins, and they needed a bigger home than this one-bedroom "starter" they loved so much. The house was in immaculate condition, only ten years old, and their price was below appraised value, only $55,000! Yet they couldn't find a buyer because the bank mortgage rates were insanely high, somewhere between 12 and 13 percent.

After six months of frustration, they met their perfect buyer. Anne Marie Fisk, 35, was a successful artist who had left her Chicago-area home because she fell in love with the work of Georgia O'Keeffe and the gorgeous New Mexico scenery and creative lifestyle. She was also recovering from a recent divorce and had a bad falling out with her parents, whom she described as rich but stingy, and an older brother who owned a car dealership and had financed a new, baby-blue van for her so she could transport her large canvases around. For Anne Marie, Santa Fe was a new beginning, a fresh start in life. And the Marshalls' adobe house suited her perfectly. Located on a stunning mesa, it offered views of pink-purple sunsets, and it had a well-lit storage shed that she could turn into a working studio.

Better yet, Anne Marie had landed an artist's job in the graphics department of a slick monthly magazine in town. She didn't have much of a down payment to make (only $5,000), but between her job and her independent art sales, she seemed easily able to make the monthly payment. The Marshalls gave her a *wraparound mortgage* for $50,000 at 10 percent and continued to pay their own mortgage on the house, with the provision that Anne Marie would need to get new financing and cash them out in five years' time. They didn't even check out her credit rating. Her payments were slightly under $500 a month.

Everything went along swimmingly and everybody was happy for the first 18 months, until Anne Marie lost her job. Actually, she quit. She claimed the art director was sexually harassing her, but he denied it and the other women in the department were too afraid of losing their jobs to come to Anne Marie's defense. She considered pursuing a court case but gave it up as too much hassle, and with too much chance of losing. Because she'd resigned "voluntarily," she didn't even qualify for unemployment compensation. She wasn't able to find another job in her field because Santa Fe is a fairly small community and opportunities were limited.

Determined to make it on freelance sales of her art, Anne Marie poured her remaining savings into remodeling the shed as a fabulous working studio. There, she turned out her colorful scenic paintings and went into a sideline with hand-designed turquoise jewelry that she took to weekend swap meets all over the Southwest.

It's not easy to make a living as a freelance artist, and, you guessed it, before long Anne Marie's mortgage payments started arriving at the Marshalls' house late, then later, then in one-half installments, then not at all.

Dwight and Jane were understanding and patient. Indeed, they liked Anne Marie and wanted nothing more than for her to keep the house and keep up the payments. They even took a small painting in lieu of the mortgage payment one month. But they were still paying their own mortgage on the house and couldn't afford to carry her indefinitely. The relationship between the Marshalls and Anne Marie became painfully strained. The monthly telephone calls were extremely stressful for both parties.

Things went from bad to worse when Anne Marie's estranged brother in Chicago sent a repossession company to take back the van, which was also behind on its payments. Without the car, she couldn't even get to the swap meets. Then she developed a mysterious and debilitating illness, a kind of allergy so fierce that she had to be rushed to the hospital in the middle of the night, struggling for breath.

The Marshalls could hardly bring themselves to foreclose on Anne Marie in her pitiful condition, but they also couldn't see what alternatives they might have if she continued to be incapable of making her payments. Every now and then, she'd sell a major painting and catch up on her past-due bills, but within a few months she'd be broke again and the unfortunate cycle of late checks and late-night phone calls would begin again.

Despite the problems, the story actually has a happy ending. By 1986, with her five-year refinancing coming due in less than a year, Anne Marie found the house was worth quite a lot more than the $55,000 she had paid in 1982, and simultaneously the national mortgage interest rates had come down and the real estate picture had brightened, with 3.5 million existing single-family homes sold. She sold the adobe home and studio for a cool $74,900 to a couple from Denver who had good credit and were able to get a bank loan.

The Marshalls got their money out of the house and paid off their original mortgage, and Anne Marie "walked" with more than $20,000 profit after paying the agent's commission and closing costs. She got a new van and was last seen heading for Colorado.

Everybody "won" in the end, but if you asked the Marshalls whether they'd ever finance a buyer again, they'd probably say no. It was just too much heartache putting up with Anne Marie Fisk and her freelance artist career. But, yes indeed they would carry owner financing again if times were tough, as in 1982, and they had to do it in order to get a sale. But they'd look for a buyer who'd held the same job for at least five years!

The Worst-Case Scenario

At least the Santa Fe artist was honest and hardworking. Barney and Joanne Metesky of Dallas had just about the worst story of seller financing we've ever heard. They were in the unfortunate position of having to sell a good, solid, two-story house in the Oak Park neighborhood of Dallas in 1987, when the economy of Texas went into a horrible slump.

It was a time when you just plain couldn't sell a house in Dallas without taking a loss, and the major oil companies were laying off thousands of workers. Barney was out of work himself, but managed to parlay his two master's degrees into a great job as curator of education at a major art museum—in Portland, Oregon. Sadly, Barney and Joanne packed up their belongings and prepared to leave Texas.

They sold the house at a sacrifice. The price was $96,000, less than the place was worth, and the buyers, Bill and DeeDee Gable, assumed their FHA mortgage of about $70,000, with Barney and Joanne carrying the balance of $26,000 in a second mortgage. That's right, the buyers got the house for nothing down *and* no credit required, and the sellers actually had to pay the agent's commission and closing costs (about $7,000 total) just to get rid of their perfectly nice home in a decent neighborhood.

It got worse. Off in Portland, the Meteskys received their monthly second mortgage payments (about $260) faithfully and thought nothing was wrong. They didn't realize the Gables were having financial difficulty and had stopped making the first (assumed) mortgage payments until they were notified by the bank that foreclosure was imminent. Hysteria ensued as they tried in vain to reach the Gables, who as it turned out had already left the home abandoned and pretty much trashed. Just to save their credit rating, Barney and Joanne had to pay all the back mortgage payments and put the house up for sale one more time.

By now, you're getting the idea. Seller financing tends to be even more available in times of depressed economy—times like now—or when either the property or the seller is in some kind of trouble. But it's also a great vehicle for the seller if the buyer is honest and keeps up the payments. Rosie Franklin never regretted selling us the farm in Vermont, and neither did that dentist in Seattle. Those were cases where the owner carried the paper and made out just fine.

If you're any kind of sincere buyer, even if your credit is just plain nonexistent, there is definitely a seller out there who's willing to finance you. Don't be afraid to approach sellers with the proposal that they finance the sale. They may turn you down in great consternation, may be insulted by the very notion. But they may also call you back a week or a month later.

You're the buyer. You're in the driver's seat. Just don't take on a payment that you can't realistically meet.

CHAPTER FIVE

Lease with Option

Considering how well it works, and considering that it's so beneficial for both buyers and sellers, it's surprising that the lease with an option to purchase is not used more often. The biggest problem seems to be that most real estate agents hate it. Their attitude is that if you lease with an option to purchase, you still haven't bought the home, and they can't collect their all-important commission. But smart agents know different, as we will demonstrate.

The lease option IS a form of purchasing, and in many cases it can be done with no credit required. Done properly, it will lead to your owning the home. It's a first step in the door of home ownership and there are many ways in which it can culminate in a title deed without requiring a visit to the lending officer.

For starters, what is a lease option? It's a contract in which the buyer agrees to rent the home for a specific period of time (usually a year), with all or part of the rent going toward the purchase of the property. Every time you make out a rent check, you increase your equity in the home and improve your chances of buying the place. The lease option contract also establishes the price of the home, so that in essence you have "frozen" the price. If, a year later, the property values in the neighborhood have improved and the house is worth more, the seller is

stuck with a year-old price, and the buyer gets a bargain. If the value of the home has gone down, however, you're not obliged to exercise your option (buy).

It's a beautiful arrangement. From the seller's
point of view, it makes the house much easier to sell,
and that's important in a slow or cold market. From
the buyer's perspective, it can make a house more
affordable, easier to get into without qualifying for
a loan, and gain some extra time in which to get financing. Indeed, by the time the buyer has paid rent
for a year and accumulated equity in the property,
a lender may be more inclined to give a mortgage
because the buyer has already made the down payment, so to speak. If the buyer has been a good tenant, always prompt with the rent check, the seller
may be persuaded to finance the purchase because
he has built up some confidence in the buyer's ability to pay. If the old mortgage is assumable, the
seller may be willing to carry a second mortgage.

There is no guarantee that the seller will carry a
second mortgage, essentially providing part of the
financing, but it makes good sense for a particular
kind of seller. If he or she doesn't absolutely need
the cash all at one time, there's a lot more profit to
be made in extending financing and collecting the
interest. Sometimes, too, a seller just doesn't want
the hassle of finding a new buyer and will extend you
a second mortgage just to complete the sale.

Indeed, some lease option contracts build up so
much value that they can actually be sold, transferred to another buyer (as long as there is not a
clause that prohibits such transfer). The lease option
is a kind of ownership because it's a legal, binding
guarantee of the right to buy a house at a set price,
with a certain amount of equity already paid in.

You'll find relatively few homes offered at lease
option terms in newspaper classified ads, but don't

be discouraged. Any house for sale may be available for lease option if you make the offer, especially if the home has been sitting unsold for a long time. Even houses for rent could be lease optioned if you can convince the landlord to sell that way.

There is usually (but not always) an option fee, a kind of modest down payment, required to get into a lease option purchase. This amount, whatever it is, is nonrefundable, so if in the end you don't buy the house, the seller is entitled to keep what you've paid in. Here's a great deal for a buyer without good credit:

Option Fee: $3,000. This is the "$3,000-moves-you-in!" pitch, as we saw with the example of Leo Carrol in Chapter One. The option payment is completely negotiable and depends on the value of the home. If it's worth $250,000, the option fee might be more like $10,000. On the other hand, there could be no option fee at all if the house is inexpensive or the seller desperate. We suggest $3,000 as a fair option fee on a house worth somewhere around $100,000. It's about 3 percent. Remember this amount, if any, is not refundable. But you don't lose it if you buy the house! It goes right toward your purchase, like a regular down payment.

Rent Applied Toward Purchase: $800 a month, 100 percent applied toward purchase. This would be a terrific deal for any buyer, but not every seller is willing to allow the entire rent to apply to the purchase. Sometimes they'll offer 80 percent, 50 percent, even 20 percent. Like the option fee, it's completely negotiable. As a buyer, you want the largest possible percentage, and preferably *all*, of your rent to go toward the sale price of the house. That way, you're not wasting a penny on rent. You're in effect already paying for the house with every rent check. At this price, $800 a month 100 percent toward purchase, in a single year you'd build up $9,600 equity in the home. Add to that the $3,000 option fee, and you've got $12,600 down payment already made. If the sale price is $100,000 or thereabouts, you're in the neighborhood of a decent down payment on the books, and it's a lot easier to accumulate a down payment with monthly rent than try to save up a bundle.

Term of the Option: one year. Some options will go for shorter periods or longer ones, but a year seems about the right amount of time. The seller feels he's not tying up the property for an inordinate amount of time; if you don't buy, he can turn around and resell or re-lease option the house in a year's time. The buyer knows he has a year in which to make sure he really wants to buy the house, to shore up his credit or find new financing, persuade the seller to finance the deal, or perhaps interest a partner or investor into coming in to help out with the purchase.

Renewal of the Option: Yes, if both parties agree. There should be a clause that allows for the option to be renewed for a second year, *but* the terms are open to negotiation and may be completely different. For one thing, the seller doesn't have to maintain the price you set in the original contract. He's got every right to increase the price, and is likely to do so if the market has improved or if the house has gone up in value. The monthly rent could go up also, and the percentage of rent applied to purchase could go down or disappear altogether. If all that sounds rather dire, just be sure to exercise your option and buy the house within the original allotted time. Once the contract expires, all terms are changeable, and you can't expect the average seller to carry a lease option indefinitely. If you have a good relationship with the seller, however, and that person is not in urgent need of closing the sale, it's possible you could negotiate a second-year renewal on agreeable terms. Your best bet: "exercise."

Transferability of the Option: Yes, from a buyer's point of view, it's desirable to have the right to transfer or sell the option to another party. Not all sellers will go along with this, because they may fear that the new holder of the option will not be reliable, or they may just plain not want to take the chance of dealing with someone they don't know and have never met. But as the buyer you want this power of transferability for some very good reasons. If your option is close to expiring and you still haven't been able to get the financing to close the sale, you could transfer the option to a friend or relative with better credit, let them buy the house, and then sell it back to you. Or, you could find that the option is worth money, quite a lot of money, to another buyer. Let's say you've already put $10,000 into the deal and you've frozen the price at a favorable, low level. Somebody could come along, pay you $10,000 to take over your option, and buy the house for themselves. You got a year's free rent and lost nothing. Maybe you'd even sell the option for $5,000, and at least get half of your investment back. Anything is better than losing what you put into the deal just because you can't exercise on time.

If all this "exercising" sounds like "financial aerobics," just remember exercise is good for you! A lease option is like paying rent without losing the rent money. We're not saying you "can't lose" because nothing in real estate is foolproof, but if the seller is willing to credit 100 percent of the rent toward the purchase, the buyer almost always exercises his or her option. With every month that passes, the buyer has more invested in the house and more incentive to complete the deal.

Right to Cancel the Lease: Yes, with 30 days' written notice, but the buyer loses all rent credit and the option fee. Some sellers don't want to give the buyer the right to cancel the lease, but most buyers will feel safer and more comfortable with the deal if they have the right to cancel at any time, on a month's notice. The seller, of course, keeps everything paid to him, and can resell or re-lease the house. You won't cancel the lease if you're happy with the house!

Agent's Commission: Yes, the agent CAN receive his or her commission on a lease option purchase, and that's something most agents need to have explained. One good way to do this is for the seller to give the agent an advance on the commission at the time the lease option is signed, with the balance to be paid when the buyer exercises the option. For example, Jack and Jill sold their house for $90,000 on a lease option, with the buyers putting up a $3,000 option fee. The agent's commission of 6 percent amounts to $5,400 on the sale, so they advanced him $1,000 out of the buyer's $3,000 option fee, with $4,400 to follow at closing. The agent was happy to get his first thousand dollars, Jack and Jill got $2,000 option fee plus monthly rent, and the buyers got a fabulous deal. If, in the end, they don't buy the house, the agents gets to keep the $1,000, and the sellers wouldn't hesitate to lease option it again.

The agent in this case learned the valuable lesson that selling a house on a lease option puts money in his pocket and sets up a mechanism that is almost certain to pay his entire commission eventually. This is far better than having the house sit unsold, producing nothing, for months on end while the agency spends money to advertise it, show it, and so forth.

But you'd be amazed at how much resistance some agents will put up against using the lease option route. We've heard stories of sellers who simply couldn't convince their agent to do it, and had to wait until the listing expired and then do it themselves without an agent, or switch to an agent who would cooperate.

Real estate agents, for the most part, are working for the seller, who pays their commission, so be aware of that. Nonetheless, a savvy agent can be a buyer's best friend! There are just as many different kinds of agents as there are different kinds of people in the world, and it's great when you find an agent you can work with.

Often, a smart agent can literally make the deal happen, even when you lack credit. Also remember that if you find an agent you like, someone who understands your needs, you can use that person as a "buyer's agent," a representative who searches out homes that meet your requirements and acts on your behalf with the sellers.

Any well-stocked stationery story will have lease option purchase forms available. The following sample contract is a good, basic one that covers the major points. Add your own clauses to reflect your personal concerns, but if you are going to create original clauses, we strongly advise that you have a competent real estate professional or attorney check your work to be sure that everything about it is legal and proper.

LEASE WITH OPTION TO PURCHASE

RECEIVED FROM: _____ (buyers) _____
hereinafter refered to as Tenant, the sum of _____
_____ dollars ($ _____)
evidenced by (check one) Cash ( ), Cashier's Check ( ),
Personal Check ( ) as a deposit which, upon acceptance
of this Lease, the Owner of the premises, hereinafter referred to as Owner, shall apply and deposit as follows:
Nonrefundable option fee: $
Rent for the period from _____ to _____ : $ _____
Security deposit: $
TOTAL: $
If Owner does not accept this Lease within three (3) days,
this deposit is to be refunded in full.
Tenant offers to lease from Owner the premises situated
in city of _____, county of _____, state of
_____, described as follows:
_____
_____

on the following terms and conditions:

1. **TERM:** The terms shall commence on _____, 19—,
and continue for a period of _____months thereafter.

2. **RENT:** Rent shall be _____dollars ($ _____) per
month, payable in advance on the _____day of the month
to Owner or his authorized agent at the following address: _____
_____

or any other address which the Owner may specify. In
the event rent is not paid within five days of due date,
Tenant agrees to pay a late charge of $ _____ plus 10 per-
cent interest per annun on the overdue amount. Tenant
also agrees to pay $ _____ for each dishonored bank check.

3. **UTILITIES:** Tenant shall be responsible for payment
of all utilities and services.

4. **USE:** Premises shall be used as a residence for no
more than _____adults and _____children.

5. **PETS:** No pets shall be brought onto the premises
without prior written consent of the Owner.

6. **TRANSFER OR ASSIGNMENT:** Tenant shall have
the right to transfer or assign this agreement or sublet

the premises to another party or parties without prior written consent of Owner.

7. **MAINTENANCE AND REPAIRS:** Tenant acknowledges the premises are in good order and repair and Tenant shall at his own expense maintain the premises in a clean and sanitary manner including all equipment, appliances, furnishings and fixtures and shall surrender the same at termination of this agreement in as good a condition as found, except for normal wear and tear. Tenant shall be responsible for any damage to premises as a result of his negligence and that of his family, invitees, or guests. Tenant shall not paint, wallpaper, or otherwise decorate premises without prior written consent of Owner. Tenant shall irrigate and maintain all landscaping, shrubs, lawns, trees, and keep the same clear of rubbish or weeds.

8. **PHYSICAL POSSESSION:** Tenant shall take physical possession of premises within three (3) days of the commencement of term hereof. Tenant shall not be liable for any rent until possession is delivered.

9. **SECURITY DEPOSIT:** Owner may but is not obliged to apply any portion of the security deposit above to Tenant's obligations, with any balance remaining to be refunded to Tenant on termination of this agreement.

10. **ENTRY AND INSPECTION:** Tenant shall permit Owner to enter and inspect premises on reasonable notice for the purpose of making repairs or showing the premises to potential tenants or purchasors.

11. **INDEMNIFICATION:** Tenant agrees to hold Owner blameless for any injury or damage to Tenant or other persons on the premises, unless such injury or damage occurs as a result of Owner's negligence or unlawful act.

12. **DEFAULT:** If Tenant shall fail to pay rent when due or perform any term hereof, after not less than three (3) days' written notice of such default given in the manner required by law, Owner may terminate all rights of Tenant hereunder unless Tenant within said time shall cure such default. If Tenant abandons or vacates the premises while in default of payment of rent, Owner may consider all property left on the premises to be abandoned and may dispose of such property in any legal manner. All property on the premises is hereby subject to lien in favor

of Owner for the payment of all sums due. In the event of a default by Tenant, Owner may elect to (a) continue the lease in effect and enforce all his rights and remedies, including the right to recover all rents due, or (b) terminate all Tenant's rights hereunder and recover from Tenant all damages incurred by reason of the breach of this lease.

13. **ATTORNEY'S FEES:** In any legal action brought by either party to enforce the terms hereof, the prevailing party shall be entitled to all costs incurred in such action, including a reasonable attorney's fee.

14. **PEST CONTROL INSPECTION:** The main building and all attached structures to be inspected by a licensed structural pest control operator prior to delivery of physical possession. Owner to pay for (1) Elimination of infestation and/or infection of wood-destroying pests or organisms, (2) Repair of damage caused by such infestation and/or infection, (3) Correction of conditions which caused said damage. Owner shall not be responsible for any work recommended to correct conditions usually deemed likely to lead to infestation or infection of wood-destroying pests or organisms, where no evidence of actual infestation is found.

15. **HEIRS AND ASSIGNS:** This lease is binding to and continues to the benefit of all heirs, assigns, or successors of the parties herein.

16. **RENTING AFTER EXPIRATION:** After the expiration of this lease, Tenant may continue renting premises with the written consent of Owner on a month to month tenancy basis, but no such tenancy after the expiration shall extend the time for the exercise of the purchase option, unless agreed to in writing by Owner.

17. **OPTION:** As long as Tenant is not in default of any terms and conditions herein, Tenant shall have the option to purchase the property herein described at a purchase price of: _____
_____ dollars ($ _____) on the following terms and conditions:
Nonrefundable option fee of $ _____ applies toward purchase. 100 percent of rent applies toward purchase. Tenant may cancel lease at any time with 30 days' written notice to Owner. If Tenant cancels lease, Tenant cancels

the purchase and forfeits the option fee and any rent credits.

If Tenant exercises option to purchase, property is to be sold in as-is condition, with no warranties or representations by Owner. Tenant shall receive a copy of the latest pest control inspection report, but Owner shall not pay for any damage whether occurring before or after the date of signing the lease option.

Monthly rent must be received by the _____th day of each month or the purchase option becomes void and any rent credit toward the purchase price is forfeited.

Second-year lease may be negotiated between Owner and Tenant, with all terms including purchase price and percentage of rent applied toward purchase negotiable.

_____
_____
_____
_____

(Note: here add any additional clauses that reflect your personal needs or the needs of the house itself. For example, you might want to have the owner agree to pay for your new carpets, or guarantee that certain appliances will stay with the property. The owner may want a clause saying the tenant is 100 percent responsible for the upkeep of the swimming pool, or other feature of the house. You or the agent can type in any clause or condition as long as the sellers will agree to it.)

18. **ENCUMBRANCES:** Tenant shall take title to the property subject to any existing covenants, conditions, restrictions, reservations, rights of way and easements of record, and any real estate taxes not yet due. The amount of any bond or assessment which is a lien shall be paid by Owner before title is transferred.

19. **PERSONAL PROPERTY:** No personal property on the premises shall be included in the purchase price, with the following exceptions: _____
_____

20. **FIXTURES:** All fixtures permanently attached to the real property shall be included in the purchase price, such fixtures to include all wallcoverings, carpets, drapes,

blinds, window and door screens, awnings, outdoor plants and trees, and _____

21. **FINANCING:** The parties acknowledge the impossibility of speculation of availability of future financing. Performance of this agreement shall not be dependent on warranties or representations by broker or Owner of financing. However, Owner agrees to consider any proposal in writing by Tenant requesting full or partial owner financing of the purchase. Owner shall not be obliged to extend any such financing.

22. **TITLE INSURANCE:** Owner agrees to present evidence of title in the form of a title insurance policy prior to Tenant's purchase of the property.*

23. **EXAMINATION OF TITLE:** Tenant shall have a period of ten (10) days from the date of the exercise of this option to examine the title to the property and report any objections to exceptions to the title. Any exceptions to the title shall be deemed accepted unless Tenant objects in writing within said ten (10) days. If Tenant objects to any exception to title, Owner shall have sixty (60) days thereafter in which to remove all such exceptions, or if such exceptions are not removed within sixty (60) days, Tenant shall have the right to terminate and end the rights and obligations hereunder unless he agrees to purchase the property subject to such exceptions.

24. **ESCROW AND CLOSING COSTS:** Escrow fees and closing costs shall be entirely paid by Owner.

25. **CLOSE OF ESCROW:** Within _____ days of exercise of the option, Owner and Tenant shall deposit with a valid escrow holder, to be chosen by Owner, all monies and instruments necessary to close escrow and complete the sale of property in accordance with all terms and conditions herein.

26. **PRORATED TAXES AND INSURANCE:** Real estate taxes and insurance premiums on the property are to be prorated between Owner and Tenant as of the date of recording of deed.

*A note on clause 22: Title Insurance. The seller should provide the buyer with a copy of his title insurance, just to prove that the title is good and clear. The buyer will also want to purchase his own title insurance policy.

27. **EXERCISE OF OPTION:** This option shall be exercised by delivering written notice to Owner prior to the expiration date of this option and by an additional payment on account of the purchase price of: *(Purchase Price minus Option Fee and Rent Credit Paid) dollars* to account of Owner to the authorized escrow holder referred to above. If mailed, the written notice shall be sent by certified mail to Owner at the address above, and shall be deemed to have been delivered on the date of postmark.

28. **EXPIRATION OF OPTION:** This option may be exercised any time after *month, day, year* and shall expire at midnight on *month, day, year*. Upon expiration Owner shall be released from all obligations and all of Tenant's rights shall cease.

The undersigned Tenant hereby acknowledges receipt of a copy of this agreement:

Dated: _____

Tenant's broker: _____   Tenant: _____
Address: _____   Address: _____
_____   _____
Phone: _____   Phone: _____

ACCEPTANCE: The undersigned Owner accepts the foregoing offer:

Broker's fee: Owner agrees to pay to *Broker's Name*, the agent in this transaction, *percentage*% of the option fee in this agreement and authorizes the agent to deduct said percentage from the deposit received. In addition, Owner agrees to pay on closing of escrow the additional sum of dollars in the event the option is exercised and the sale completed. In the event that legal action is instituted to collect this fee, Owner agrees to pay reasonable attorney's cost.

The undersigned Owner hereby acknowledges receipt of a copy of this agreement:

Dated: _____

Owner's broker: _____   Owner: _____
Address: _____   Address: _____
Phone: _____   Phone: _____

Option-al Optimism

As with our personal real estate contract in Chapter Four, this lease option agreement is a simple one, with just the essential clauses included. (Some pre-printed option forms are even simpler.) The most important clauses in our version are clause 6, "transfer or assignment," and clause 21, "financing." One or the other of these clauses could help you close the sale and exercise the option even without adequate credit.

As we mentioned earlier, the ability to transfer or assign the option could be an important factor, because you could assign it to another party whose credit is good enough to get a mortgage, and who is willing to share equity with you or resell the property back to you. Your valid option is in itself a kind of partial ownership with tangible value as long as the option is exercised before the expiration date.

Clause 21 doesn't obligate the seller to finance the purchase, but it does leave that door slightly open. Here is your chance to establish credit with the seller even if you have none with the bank. If you pay your rent on time faithfully, the seller will gradually come to trust your honesty and ability to pay. After a year of building up that kind of fiduciary trust, you may be able to convince the seller to finance the sale or at least carry some of the paper. A reasonable down payment will help a lot to sweeten the deal.

Sellers and buyers are only human, after all. In many cases, the seller will be so grateful for a lease option tenant who pays rent on time that he'll do everything possible to make it easier for you to complete the purchase. And you as the tenant have enough time to figure out everything about the house and whether you really want to own it. If you're late on the rent one month, the seller has the right to take away your option and all your rent credit, but many sellers will find the patience to forgive the delay if you catch up with the rent promptly and have a good excuse for being late. Not every clause has to be rigidly enforced to the letter of the law, but you should not enter into this or any agreement if you're not confident you can live up to its every requirement.

Tenants are often the most likely people to buy a home. For starters, they're already in residence and it's easier to stay put than to move. You're in a great position to buy the home you live in on a lease option if one or more of the following conditions applies:

• The landlord has become a personal friend and decides to sell the house, offering it first to you before putting it on the market.

• You're on a job promotion track that is likely to lead to more income in the future than you have now, or you're about to graduate from a professional school with a degree that will lead to new job opportunities.

• You're gradually paying off debts and expect your credit rating to improve in the near future (and you're carefully checking into that rating to make sure it reflects your payments).

• The landlord encounters financial difficulties of his or her own, such as medical emergency, divorce, loss of employment, or adverse legal judgments.

• The landlord dies and the heirs to the estate need to liquidate property for tax or other reasons.

• Or, your parent or relative dies and you suddenly come into a once-in-a-lifetime inheritance, which doesn't have to be huge—just big enough to constitute an irresistible down payment offer to your landlord.

Margaret and Jim Lewis bought their first home in Madison, Wisconsin, just because they happened to be living in it when the owner decided to sell. They never thought they could qualify for a mortgage, with Jim's earnings as an assistant professor at the university being gobbled up each month with little to spare, while Margaret cared for their three children and made a few dollars on the side selling her homemade quilts.

They had one thing going for them, however, when the elderly landlady decided it was time to sell the house. They'd been renting there for almost ten years, and had never been more than a week late paying the rent.

In fact, they were forced to either buy the house or move, and they loved the place so much—and hated the idea of moving all their belongings and maybe having to place the kids in a new school district—that they took out a lease option and decided to at least try their best to complete the sale. The landlady had grown to like Jim and Margaret a lot and even considered their children as surrogate grandchildren for whom she baked cookies and sent birthday cards.

The lease option required no option fee at all, and their rent went up only $100 a month, but Jim and Margaret had only a year in which to finance the purchase. They found an astonishing motivation, however, in the simple fact that every rent check was increasing their down payment. Jim found that his teacher's credit union open to employees at the University of Wisconsin was far more liberal than any conventional bank lender, and Margaret took a job as a cashier in the campus bookstore to supplement their income. But in the end—with just a month to spare—they squeaked by and got the credit union home mortgage. The union officer told Jim it was possible only because the lease option had given them a substantial down payment, and locked in a great price, so that the house itself was worth 30 percent more than the loan.

Jim and Margaret's experience shows one way in which a rental property can be turned over into a lease option purchase. Taking a page from their book, you can forget about the houses listed for sale and instead go out looking at houses for rent. Find a rental you like and offer the landlord to lease option it. You have nothing to lose, and you'd be surprised at the number of landlords who might be interested.

Charlie Merriweather, a newly single guy in his thirties, had an otherworldly experience with rental-turned-option in the early 1980s in Sacramento, California. Divorced and desolate, he was sleeping on a friend's couch, his belongings locked in a public storage place, when he ran into the Mad Rabbi in the religion section of a bookstore. They struck up a conversation about the Old Testament, although Charlie wasn't particularly religious. The pain of divorce had sent him running into the arms of any spiritual consolation he could find, however.

At any rate, after some soul-searching talk, the Mad Rabbi asked Charlie where he lived, and after hearing the sad tale of his homelessness, offered to rent Charlie a small house in the north end of town with an option to purchase it.

This was some kind of bolt from the blue, not likely to happen to anyone, but nonetheless a true story. Charlie investigated the house and found it was a fabulous 1930s Sacramento bungalow with fireplace, carpets, upstairs bedrooms for his kids, a fenced backyard with fish pond, sloping floors, leaded glass windows, on a very busy street but set back 75 feet from the sidewalk. A great place for a single dad, and it was clean, the heat was on, the refrigerator cold and gas range operational. The mad thing about the house, and the reason why Charlie called the rabbi the Mad Rabbi, was that the property had been sitting there empty, unrented, and not for sale, for more than a year, with full utilities on and a cleaning lady coming over now and then. There was no key to the house, but you could get in by entering through the back door of the garage.

The rabbi owned dozens of such houses; they made him feel secure. He never advertised them, just waited for the "right" person to come along. He specialized in helping down and out people who had enough resources to pay the rent. The deal he offered Charlie was $550 a month rent to accrue over a year to a down payment of $6,600, after which time Charlie could buy the house for about $40,000, with the rabbi's financing.

It was a deal made in Heaven with the full blessing of the prophets, but Charlie blew it. He started drinking heavily, fell behind in the rent, lost the confidence of the rabbi (who got *really* "mad" when he didn't get his check), and eventually packed everything he could carry into his car and left Sacramento for some place—anyplace—where he could start a new life. Divorce will do that to people.

But before leaving the house, Charlie turned the place over to a family of four, friends who had been looking for a place to rent. He didn't have any authority to let other people live in the house, but he knew this family was responsible and would pay the rabbi promptly, and since they were also Jewish he figured the rabbi would like them. Astonishingly enough, it worked out well. The family took over the house and the lease option, always paid the rabbi on time and, so to speak, lived happily ever after.

Lease option deals aren't limited to low-cost, old,

or unwanted properties. In the early 1990s, we find houses offered for lease option in the $200,000 to $400,000 range. If you look under the special category "Rent to Own" in the classifieds, you may find that the houses offered are the better and more expensive ones, in fact. But that doesn't mean you can't approach an owner in a lower price range. Most people simply don't think of listing their property as "Rent to Own."

One kind of property that is readily adaptable to the lease option idea is the luxury condominium, and it's time we looked at one, just as an example. When Carolyn Yamamoto was having trouble selling her plush condo in the Hollywood Hills in 1990, she finally succeeded by leasing it with an option. The place had a swimming pool, shared by six apartments, with a breathtaking view of Los Angeles from the San Bernardino Mountains to the sea. There was an eight-person hot tub, a laundry room, and secured parking under the building, plus her apartment featured cathedral ceilings, two fireplaces, two baths, a dazzling view from the living room, formal dining room, and modern kitchen. Everything about this condo was luxurious and modern. The price was $189,000, exactly what Carolyn herself had paid for it two years earlier.

But, after all that, it had only one bedroom, and the rules of the condo association prohibited children and dogs. Carolyn was up against the age-old problem that most buyers don't want a one-bedroom condo. The type of people who buy a home usually need more space than that, and frequently have children. She needed a special buyer, and after months of frustration with no sale, she found Randy and Jamie, a middle-aged couple with two cats, who lease optioned the condo for $1,200 a month with no option fee, but they did pay an extra month's rent in advance as a security deposit.

That deal worked out fine for everyone. Carolyn was able to move on to her new job in San Francisco, while Randy and Jamie took good care of the condo and in fact became popular social hosts in the building, getting along well with the other condo occupants. Their credit was shaky, but after a year they managed to swing a mortgage with a down payment borrowed from Randy's parents, because they effectively paid less for the condo than it was worth three years earlier when it was brand new.

That tells you something about condos, by the way. Compared with single-family homes, they do not appreciate much in value, and you can't add rooms or remodel/redesign a condo to increase its worth as you can with a detached home. Most people want a real home, not an apartment, when they buy real estate, but condos make sense if you live in a major urban area or you're retired and tired of maintaining a yard or big house, or if you're simply a busy person who hates housework.

You can also regard a condo as a "starter," just something to get you out of renting and into real property until you can "roll over" (IRS lingo for selling your home and buying another) into a real house. And condos are available on a lease option basis, no credit required, in virtually every city in the nation. Some are even nothing down, "just take over payments." Just be careful!

CHAPTER SIX

The 30/70 Rule

It's not a rule, or at least we haven't been able to find it written down anywhere, and no banker would admit to it as a hard-and-fast guideline, but it's a common practice in lending circles that if you can put 30 percent of the price of a house as a down payment, the lender will issue a mortgage for the remaining 70 percent, even if you don't have good credit.

The reasoning is simply that anyone who pays 30 percent into a house is highly unlikely to walk away from the investment. It's a real commitment, and eliminates the necessity of a good credit rating. And if the bank should be forced to foreclose on the mortgage, presumably the home will be worth a great deal more than the amount owed on it.

Of course, the house itself has to be worth the amount of the sale price or this "rule" would be meaningless. The bank or lending agency may insist on qualifying the property through some official assessment or appraisal, but once the value of the home is established and you're able to put 30 percent or more of that value down, you should be able to get a mortgage even if you've had past credit problems or have no credit at all.

There is no better example of this than our old friend, Patty Callahan in Cambria, California. Patty would be the first to admit that her credit was just plain awful. She had a drinking problem in the 1970s and 1980s, which she has since recovered from completely, and today she is a sober and proud attorney specializing in family and child custody disputes.

But when Patty arrived in Cambria from her childhood home in Seattle in 1970, she was a little wild. She had a daughter out of wedlock and decided to raise the child herself, which wasn't easy on the salary of a substitute schoolteacher, her profession at the time. Patty and babe moved into a bohemian cabin in the woods along the Big Sur coast during a time when such digs could be had cheaply. They raised chickens and dozens of other animals in a horribly unkempt yard—one neighbor dubbed Patty's chicken coop "Animal Auschwitz"—and seemed to live on the sun in the morning and the moon at night. That, and large quantities of frozen vodka.

Inside, the house was the messiest place anyone had ever seen, even in disheveled Big Sur circles. Patty hung a wooden sign reading "Disorderly Room" over her mantel. She never did the dishes until there was nothing clean left to eat or drink from. Laundry was tossed on the floors, in heaps. She lavished love and attention on her child, however, and the little girl was never neglected. The Callahan gals had a free and easy lifestyle.

When Patty needed money, she'd simply write a check, whether or not there were funds in her account. She bounced checks all over the central coast until she was kicked out of every bank in town and even the teachers' credit union. Those few establishments foolish enough to give Patty a credit card soon came to regret it. She ran up massive debts in restaurants, clothing stores, and liquor stores until the cards were repossessed, and never bothered to make a payment. She was *not* a thief and not dishonest, and eventually had to repay every one of the bad checks and credit card bills. She was just a young person who had no sense of responsibility about money.

Eventually, Patty met the person she'd needed all along to keep her on the straight and narrow path. The kindly Mrs. Chin, a professional bookkeeper, agreed to take over Patty's financial affairs for nothing more than love and affection for Patty and her daughter. After that, all Patty's salary went directly to Mrs. Chin, who in turn paid Patty's bills and doled out small amounts of cash for Patty's gas and liquor expenses. Patty was not allowed to write a check or use a credit card. In time, the bills got paid, but her credit rating was a disaster. The mere mention of Patty's name would set every computer in California to screaming, beeping red lights.

If you knew Patty's background, all of this was even more bizzare. Her father was a wealthy doctor in Seattle. Her siblings were all doctors, lawyers, and Indian chiefs, so to speak. The family was socially prominent and respectable as could be. They lavished gifts on Patty's young daughter, who always had new clothes and toys and good health care, but they wouldn't give Patty any actual cash because they knew she'd blow it. She was the rebel, the black sheep of the family. Every few years, her father would give her a car, but hold the title himself so she couldn't sell the vehicle. She drove in Big Sur for 20 years with Washington state license plates.

In the late 1980s, Patty's father died. Her mother had already passed away, and each of the doctor's children came into a substantial inheritance.

This was the moment Patty had been waiting for. Without batting an eyelash, she picked out a fabulous $300,000 home in an upper-middle-class neighborhood of Cambria, and walked into a bank with a down payment of $100,000. She got the mortgage, of course, despite her disastrous credit rating, and overnight went from being a hippie in a cabin to a law student in a handsome five-bedroom, three-bath Cambria charmer.

The new house didn't make Patty a better housekeeper, but she finally could afford to have a cleaning lady to come in twice a week. She rented out her extra bedrooms and her little studio in the backyard to fellow law students, seasonal visitors, any decent tenant who could help her with the mortgage payments. Of course, Mrs. Chin still wrote the checks. And—you guessed it—merely owning the fine house gave Patty excellent credit!

You don't have to inherit money to buy a house on the 30/70 rule, but some kind of windfall like that certainly helps, and a lot of people do experience a once-in-a-lifetime financial boost. Maybe you'll win the lottery, or have a highly successful business project. But a bank will be even more impressed if you manage to save that 30 percent down payment through regular and methodical savings.

"The underlying principle is that a bank's perceived risk is higher with a person who doesn't have good credit," says Lynne Susman Ballew, vice president of the Tokai Bank in San Diego, a lender that provides home financing. "But if they look at you and you've managed to save up a 30 percent down payment, they may say, 'Well, the buyer doesn't have credit but they've saved a lot of money,' and issue the mortgage.

"Is the 30/70 rule a practice? Well, yes, it's a practice but it's not a rule so much as it's just basic banking sense," she continued. "The bank will look at the house itself, and if the bank is interested in investing in that property, it may issue the loan even though the buyer's credit isn't excellent. A person with very good credit can get a 90 percent loan. But a 70 percent or lower loan is considered safe because if it ever had to repossess the property, the bank figures it could get its money back.

"Of course, the bank is going to look at everything more closely because of the buyer's lack of credit. That's part of the perceived risk factor," Ballew adds. "But when you ask if a person can get a 70 percent loan despite bad credit, I'd have to say yes—sometimes."

For the sake of easy numbers, let's assume the house you want to buy costs $100,000, so the down payment you'd need to employ the 30/70 rule is $30,000. Short of robbing a bank, where could you get $30,000? Joking aside, this is exactly the way most people would implement a 30/70 no-credit purchase: determine the down payment needed, then find a way to raise it. If you have generous parents or good friends who can afford it, you could perhaps borrow the down payment on your personal "good name." Be advised, though, that a bank or lender will not be pleased to learn that you have borrowed the down payment, especially if you sign a note promising to repay it on some established schedule. It's far better if the down payment comes from a source—any source—that doesn't require repayment, such as inheritance, savings, selling your prized antique classic automobile, cashing in some stock, gambling winnings (why not?), a huge insurance settlement or lawsuit proceeds, or just an outright gift.

Remember, there's no law saying that you must divulge where you got the money, but on the other hand it's definitely illegal to misrepresent your finances in a fraudulent way. So if you have indeed borrowed the down payment and signed a promissory note to repay the loan, you must admit that in dealings with the bank. More than likely, that loan will also be a lien against the property in case you can't repay it, much like a second deed of trust. In a case where you borrow the down payment of 30 percent and then borrow the remaining 70 percent from a bank or lender, you're in effect getting 100 percent financing. It happens!

Parents, living or dead, are probably the most likely source of cash for a down payment. That's because in today's economy, most young adults can no longer afford to buy that first home without some help. The previous generation was actually better off than the current one, and our children will inherit a vast national debt and even worse financing problems.

Gifts or loans from parents aren't always advisable and don't always go smoothly, so beware. Just read "Dear Abby" or "Ann Landers" for firsthand accounts from estranged parents who loaned their children money, never got repaid, and came to resent it. Brothers and sisters will also sometimes become resentful if a parent gives a large real estate down payment to one child while not offering equal amounts to the siblings.

But parents usually want to see all their children do well, and if you're lucky enough to have parents willing and able to help you buy a home, consider yourself blessed.

It's good to know, in any case, that if you can somehow scrape up a 30 percent down payment, your lack of credit will not stand in the way of buying property.

CHAPTER SEVEN

Adverse Possession

It takes only 5 years in California, but a full 30 years in Texas, to gain legal title to property through adverse possession, a kind of legal "theft." Every state had adverse possession laws, so check with your state's Department of Real Estate for the requirements in your vicinity.

Adverse possession is simply the acquisition of real estate by occupying it and paying the property tax on it. If it seems incredible that anyone could gain property that way, be assured that it happens thousands of times every year.

Not only is no credit required, but no payments to the previous owner are required, either. Adverse possession is like "squatting," except that it's legal and you get title eventually.

This works mostly with real estate that has been abandoned by its rightful owner. Adverse possession laws exist on the books to encourage property to be used, not sit vacant. Of course there are stringent rules that must be followed, and all states require that your adverse use of the property must be:

• Open
• Continuous, for the minimum number of years in your state
• Notorious, in other words obvious

• Hostile, in other words, without permission from the owner

• And, you *must* pay the property taxes, even if someone else is also paying them

If there is an existing mortgage on the house that no one else is paying, then you must pay that too, of course, or the mortgage holder will get the property in foreclosure. But paying the mortgage is not one of the legal requirements for adverse possession, whereas paying the taxes is.

After meeting all these conditions, you can then sue in state court and be granted full title, even though you haven't paid for the house and have no credit.

Most successful adverse possession occurs in remote rural areas, where the rightful property owner may forget about or simply ignore his real estate for years. But there are also cases on record where urban property in major cities changes hands through adverse possession.

So where do you find these free houses? You look for property that has clearly been abandoned for one reason or another. Perhaps the owner is serving a long jail term in Mexico, or has moved to another state following a bitter divorce, or has suffered amnesia and is wandering around the back streets of a major city with other homeless people. Anything is possible. Some property owners are simply eccentric, mentally ill, senile, or have no one else to protect their interests. Some owners literally forget that they own the property and can't be found, no matter how hard you try.

In any case, once you find a house that's clearly unoccupied and abandoned, the law permits you to move in, start paying the taxes, and begin your waiting term of adverse possession. You don't even need to contact the owner, *but* if the rightful owner appears or contacts you and orders you to leave the premises, you have no right to stay. In short, all an owner has to do to protect himself against adverse possessors is to check his property, or have a representative check it, once in a while.

We've seen adverse possession work successfully twice in the last ten years, both times in California. One house was a crack cocaine "shooting gallery," a drug haven abandoned by its owners to tough street gangs in East Los Angeles. Brave neighbor Dave Santiago moved in, fought off the gangs, and claimed the house on Shamrock Street for his growing family. Who wants an abandoned drug den? you might ask. But the other case was a truly handsome oceanfront home in Pacific Grove, a dilapidated Victorian that was crumbling away but had inherent value because of its superb architecture and location close to the beach. The owner was a stubborn old man living in a wilderness trailer in Watsonville, who received mail at a post office box and utterly refused to do anything about the vacant house. Before adverse possession, the Australian couple who wound up getting the property had written to the owner and attempted to rent or buy the house, but he never replied and never visited the place. One stormy night, they just moved into the house rather than sleep on the beach. They figured they had nothing to lose.

You *can* lose in adverse possession, of course. Suppose you've been living in the house, paying the taxes, for four and a half years. In that time, you've spent thousands of dollars fixing up the place, installing new hardwood floors, replacing the leaky roof, and such. The rightful owner can come back from the dead, or Beirut, or wherever, and reclaim his house, and you would have no rights to it. Your investment would have been wasted, although you did get free rent for years.

If adverse possession is risky, it is also tantalizing. Imagine owning a house for practically nothing, only the taxes, just by taking it over! To enhance your eligibility, make sure you keep meticulous records and can prove the five major points:

• **Open.**   Your occupancy must be open; it cannot be secretive. The Australian couple on the beach lived in the house without curtains or shades on the living room windows, so that any passerby could observe them when they were sitting in their living room, enjoying the splashy ocean views. Dave Santiago in East L.A. kept lights burning in his front windows all night.

• **Notorious.**   This takes "open" a step further. It just means that your occupancy is obvious and blatant. Park your car in the driveway, sit on your rocker on the front porch, receive mail, open utility accounts, have a phone listed in your own name at your adverse address.

• **Continuous.**   You can't get title if you've moved back and forth from the house. You must stay there more or less all the time, keep it as your only principal residence, for the minimum number of years your state requires.

• **Hostile.**   You must *not* have the owner's permission to stay in the house. If you're staying there with permission, you will never qualify to own the house by adverse possession.

• **Pay the taxes.**   The taxes assessed on real property are a matter of public record. Find out how much the taxes are on your adverse address, then pay that amount to the county when due. Keep receipts and records of every payment. There have been cases of people who adversely occupied property for 20 years or more but could not gain title, because they didn't pay the taxes.

Finally, after you have met all these conditions, go to court and sue for **quiet title**, so named because it passes from the previous owner to you "quietly," without the former owner being notified.

Many an owner has been startled or distressed to find that his real estate no longer belongs to him. It has been "stolen" by adverse possession, and this kind of "theft" is completely legal and above board. Once the title has been transferred by the court, the property belongs to the adverse possessor "forever," until her or she sells it, passes it along to heirs or assigns, or loses it by neglect to the next adverse possessor to come along!

Although most real estate transactions don't require the services of a lawyer, adverse possession is one area in which you can't be too careful. Get a competent real estate attorney to handle your documentation.

An Ongoing Adversarial Affair

A small house on Polk Street in San Francisco has been driving real estate agents crazy for the past year or more. Some creative soul took an ordinary two-bedroom cottage and remodeled it to resemble the pyramids of Egypt, with a conical roof line and a burnt umber paint job. The house is either hideous or wonderful, depending on your taste, but it's certainly unusual, and everyone who gets past the thick bushes in the front yard to see it has some comment about it.

At one time, the owner, a single man in his forties, put it up for sale, but the real estate listing expired after four months. The agency is not allowed to sell the house without a current listing, but the owner simply disappeared. Letters to his last known address are returned. His last phone number is disconnected.

It's been 18 months since he vanished, and meanwhile a number of brave buyers have wanted to purchase the house, but couldn't. At this moment a radical coalition of activists for the homeless are conducting a formal adverse possession of the property as an overnight shelter for street people.

There is some suspicion that the owner may have died of AIDS, a victim of society's disapproval who chose to go out anonymously rather than confess to having the disease. But that is pure speculation. He could just as likely have embezzled a million dollars and fled to Argentina. One thing for sure is that the house is free and clear of any mortgage balance, and the taxes were not paid last year. If the homeless activists simply pay up the overdue taxes, they can move in with a clear conscience, unless or until the rightful owner comes back.

Prescriptive Easements

Another, less dramatic form of adverse possession is the prescriptive easement, in which the owner of the property loses rights to it by allowing someone else to use it over a number of years. The classic example is the neighbor who regularly walks or drives across your property to get to his own. If he does so without permission for the required number of years, he could get a permanent prescriptive easement giving him the right to use that land.

This kind of thing also comes up in fence and border disputes. If your neighbor puts up a fence that is actually 12 inches over on your side of the property line and you don't complain about it, he could eventually own a prescriptive easement on that extra foot of territory.

Prescriptive easements are another way of acquiring real estate without credit, but adverse possession offers the possibility of the whole ball of wax—a house that is yours for the taking. Find a ghost town out in the Wild West, a burned-out brick town house in the central city, or just some eccentric property that has been left vacant and unattended, and you could be in. At any rate, there's no landlord demanding rent.

How Can it Be that Easy?

Well, it's not, really. Adverse possession takes a number of years to culminate in a legal transfer of ownership and includes a lot of risk. It's not easy, but it's possible. Remember, however:

• **A vacant house is not necessarily abandoned.** The truly abandoned property is a rarity. You don't want to be charged with trespassing illegally on someone else's property. Before even thinking of taking adverse possession of a house, you should make every effort to locate the rightful owner. If such a person can be found, the chances are slim to none that he or she will allow you to take title by adverse possession. With most successful adverse possessions, the property is literally abandoned.

• **The laws vary from state to state.** Look into the regulations in your state by contacting the state Department of Real Estate or asking a competent professional realtor or attorney.

• **Keep impeccable records and stay strictly within the law.** The law may allow you to take adverse possession, but if the rightful owner asks you to leave, you have no right to stay.

CHAPTER EIGHT

Equity Sharing

You've heard about it. It's the newest trend in real estate, a direct result of the spiraling values of the 1980s. It's also a fine way to acquire property without adequate credit to qualify for a mortgage. It's equity sharing, or simply the sharing of the ownership of real property between several parties.

Some cities now have "equity share" as a category in the classified listings, so popular has this phenomenon become.

The classic ad: "NO QUALIFY!! Stop wasting your money on rent! Make the mortgage payment on new and resale houses throughout the area, receive 50% ownership, plus tax benefits, with zero down. Call Broker xxx-xxxx."

Too good to be true? The good news is that it works, at least for some people some of the time. A few examples:

1. One party puts up the down payment and credit, while the other invests sweat. In this case, an investor with good credit and some cash on hand swings the purchase, while the person without credit or a down payment actually lives in the house, fixes it up, and pays 100 percent of the mortgage payments. It's called "sweat equity" because these houses are usually fixer-uppers that both parties have agreed will be renovated and, eventually, resold at a profit.

Done right, this system works beautifully. You need to find a house that is cheap because it needs work, in a neighborhood that is decent and likely to improve in value. Often, the work involved is merely cosmetic—paint, wallpapers, carpets, landscaping, cleanup, and basic repairs. If the house needs fundamental, constructive work such as foundation repair, a new roof, replacement plumbing or electricity, you're almost certainly going to need professional help, and you should find out in advance exactly what it's going to cost.

Of course, you also need to find an investor rich enough (and smart enough) to put up the down payment and qualify for the mortgage. Certain real estate brokers now make a specialty of "marrying" these investors with good sweat-equity folks who can be counted on to make the mortgage payment and enhance the value of the property.

Why would an investor want to do this? There are a few excellent reasons. First of all, there are many possible tax advantages that may be attractive to a person in an upper-income bracket. Doctors are notorious for their real estate investments. More important than tax advantage, however, is the prospect of eventual, perhaps tremendous, profit. And all the while, the investor doesn't have to do a lick of work or pay a dime of the mortgage payments.

The investor and the sweat-equity buyer come to a formal agreement that their property will be resold in a specific number of years. Three to five years is a good standard, because it typically takes that long for a house to appreciate in value significantly, although some people turn a property around in only a year or two.

When the home is sold, both the investor and the

sweat-equity owner/occupant should come away with a tidy profit. That money, plus the fact that you've been making regular mortgage payments for several years, may improve your credit situation quite a bit. Even if it doesn't, you will have effectively gotten a start in home ownership, stopped paying rent, picked up the tax benefits, and made your own work and monthly payments produce a return for **you**, instead of the landlord.

Half a loaf *is* better than none!

2. Both parties occupy the property in a shared living arrangement. This works best with a duplex, where each party in the equity sharing arrangement has a private and equally good place to live, but the possibilities are endless. Perhaps the house has a granny unit, or mother-in-law apartment, or a small studio cottage in the backyard. One investor, the one who put up the greater share of the down payment, could live in the house, while the other lives in the smaller unit.

Or perhaps one party puts up the entire down payment while the other puts up his or her good credit to qualify for the mortgage, then both parties pay equal shares of the monthly payment.

Everything is negotiable with a shared living arrangement, including the percentage of equity and monthly payment. If you live in the tiny backyard cottage while the other party gets the big four-bedroom house, you might realistically be expected to pay less.

A shared living arrangement makes sense in today's market simply because real estate in many parts of the country has become too expensive for most people. The statistics on housing affordability are frightening. But if you're going to share living quarters with another buyer, naturally you must be sure that you can get along. If you go to bed early and lead a quiet life, you might not be happy with neighbors who party noisily till dawn. It's best to find out as much as possible about your partners before entering into a shared living situation.

3. The seller becomes your equity partner. This really is the wave of the future and is happening right now in every part of the country. When a seller is desperate to get out from under a mortgage payment and the house hasn't sold, it may be to his advantage to sell 50 percent equity in the property to any buyer who will take over the payments. Usually, the deal is cut for a period up to five years, after which you must either buy out the seller or resell the home.

There is rarely a cash down payment involved, and absolutely no qualifying credit is required, but the seller may insist that you pay the closing costs and the agent's commission, since the seller is getting no money up front and can't be expected to actually pay money to sell his home.

You don't need a new mortgage because you just pay the seller's existing mortgage payment, based completely on his or her credit. Sometimes this will give you a low monthly payment because it's an older mortgage. But of course you're buying only half the house, half the equity, and within three to five years you must refinance, buy out your partner, or sell and move on.

You acquire a house where the seller gets only the relief of freedom from the payments, and won't see his cash out of it for years to come. So you need to find a seller whose back is to the wall, someone who has already moved or who simply can't afford to make the payments. Unfortunately, sellers like that are more common these days. Their misfortune could be your door to financial independence.

Remember, however, that you're buying only half the house while paying the full mortgage payment, and that within five years your back could be to the wall, too, if you can't sell or refinance the house. Try to find something with an excellent prospect for improving in value.

4. Group purchase, or "hui" plan. Sometimes a group of people get together and buy real estate, property on which some of them may live, whereas others simply hold an investment share. In Hawaii, this kind of group is called a **hui**, and is a common occurrence, because land values are staggeringly high and the smallest "little grass shack" may be worth millions.

There are endless variations on group purchasing. During the "back to the land movement" of the late 1960s and 1970s, we saw a large number of communes formed, groups who bought houses and land in rural areas and lived there together. People thought the communes were a radical idea, but actually such intentional communities have long existed in American history, dating back to the Shakers and Amish people.

A modern adaptation is a corporation, a nonprofit membership association formed to purchase real estate. Each member holds stock in the corporation and a share of the property. The stock can be sold to another party, but usually the corporation bylaws will insist on membership approval of any new person joining the group, or you may be required to offer to sell your stock back to the corporation and its members before offering it to anyone else.

The group purchase can be an excellent way for

you to get at least a piece of real property ownership without needing personal credit. Typically, the corporation or group is granted the mortgage, not the individual investors. If you expect to live on the property, that arrangement must be in writing and absolutely specific.

The ideal group purchase situation might be a rural setting where there is enough land and houses for everyone who wants to live there to have a personal domicile, but the same principle can be applied to urban living through membership cooperatives. Some co-op apartment buildings in New York City have been doing it successfully for years.

In a way, a condominium building is a kind of group purchase, with membership association and communal upkeep fees, but when you buy a condo, you are buying a particular and individual space, and some credit may be required to qualify for the mortgage. In a true group purchase, your personal credit is not the foundation for the loan.

In short, if you have some good friends who are as eager as you are to stop paying rent, get your group together and buy! Many hands make light work, and you could be amazed at the power of numbers. Just be sure you really like the others, and have an inviolable personal living space guaranteed.

5. Time share.   Time-share properties are usually in resort areas, and your investment buys only a few weeks a year of residential privileges. It's certainly a form of equity sharing, because you can sell this property interest to another party, but it's not home ownership. It's vacation home ownership.

We don't recommend time shares, because they can be overpriced and difficult to resell. But if you're sure that you want to vacation in the same place every year, a time share can buy you a stable place to stay.

Equity Sharing: The Wild West

Don Donahue is a real estate broker in fashionable Marin County, California, just north of San Francisco, where home prices are so high that equity sharing has become the New Wave. He tells many amusing stories of people who have succeeded in buying an equity share, but most of them have no ending. They are happy stories as far as they go, but it remains to be seen what their final outcomes may be.

Mary Jane and Bill Monette, for example, bought a 50 percent share in a lovely, four-bedroom, two-and-a-half bath Spanish-style house in the upscale community of San Rafael. The house was priced at over $350,000, but the Monettes paid literally no down payment and required no credit, which was just as well since Bill had declared bankruptcy when his small software development company in Alameda went belly up a year earlier.

They did pay all the costs of closing the deal and all the agent's commission, so it cost them well over $20,000 to get into the house, and they took on a hefty $3,000 a month mortgage payment. Mary Jane's excellent job as public relations coordinator for a group of Napa wineries earned them enough to keep up the payments, but they quickly became house rich and cash poor. Gone are the weekend flights to Utah for skiing. Bill and Mary Jane now stay home and play Monopoly, and have their friends over for cheese, crackers, and (complimentary) Napa wine.

Nonetheless, they are living in grand style in what

had been the home of a top San Francisco import car dealer. They have a redwood sauna, small lap pool, distant view of the lights twinkling over the bay and the great span of the Golden Gate Bridge. They have Persian rugs and three fireplaces and two Airedales. And Bill is launching a new business in personalized greeting cards, installing computer-run machines that allow customers to create their own sentiments on a printed card.

The only hitch is that their clock started running in 1990 and runs out in 1995, and by 1992 they were already starting to get worried. That is, under the agreement they struck with the sellers, they have five years in which to enjoy the house, after which they must either buy out the original owners' half interest or sell the house and split the proceeds 50/50 with the people they bought from.

If they can't make a profit selling the place and can't get the credit to buy out their equity partners, it's difficult to say what Bill and Mary Jane will do.

As for the sellers, they were delighted when the Monettes purchased the equity share, because they'd simply exhausted their resources keeping up with the high mortgage payment and staggering utilities and hidden costs of maintaining such a nice home. The place just about demanded a gardener and housekeeper, unless you were home all day with nothing to do but housework. The sellers were happily installed in an inexpensive apartment in Berkeley, with most of their belongings in a self-storage unit in Oakland, vastly relieved to be free of the mortgage burden and other costs of the home.

"That's the funny thing about some of these equity sharing deals," says agent Don. "You can get into a really fantastic home for nothing down and with no credit, because the sellers just plain flat out can't afford to keep up their payments and they can't find a regular buyer either in this slow market. Some of these properties are blue ribbon, the best. And they'll let anybody in there who can cover their butts on that mortgage payment."

Anybody? Yes, anybody with money. Credit doesn't matter.

Pros and Cons of Sharing Equity

There's no question that equity sharing can be a terrific device for the renter lacking good credit who wants to get into home ownership. There are pitfalls and dangers, however, and you can't be too careful in making sure that all the details are handled in a legal and proper fashion that protects your interests.

The contract between you and the seller, entering into an equity sharing agreement or partnership, should be checked by an attorney experienced in real estate matters. In most real estate transfers, a lawyer's services are not required, but in this case we strongly urge you to get professional advice before putting your money on the line.

Owning property (even if it's only a half interest) tends to improve your credit rating, so it's possible if you share equity that you may see your credit rating rise. This is a tendency, not a rule. If you have judgments against you or old bills left unpaid, they will remain on your credit report and no amount of home ownership will make them disappear.

In any sharing arrangement that is based on the idea that you will sell the home in a specific number of years and split the proceeds, you are running a calculated risk. What if some unforseeable change occurs that makes the house impossible to sell?

What if the house actually goes down in value over the time elapsed? It could happen.

Take a calculated risk, but not a foolish one. Make sure that legal title is correctly transferred ("vested") into your name, and duly recorded in your county recorder's office. Study the values and comparable prices of other houses in the neighborhood, and inquire into the trend of real estate prices in the vicinity. Have prices been stagnant, going up, going down?

More than that, look into the greater external factors that might affect the future value of the home. Is there a major highway or other large construction project planned nearby? Is your view obstructable should someone put up a high building across the street? What is the quality of the school district, and how healthy is the local employment market? These are gravely important considerations when you are, in effect, betting that you can sell the house for a profit in x year's time. Even the nicest house could be difficult to sell if there are no jobs in the town.

Most important, be sure you know the person(s) with whom you are planning to enter into this partnership. We are basically positive about equity sharing; it's a good idea in some circumstances, but we've also heard horror stories from people who bought real estate with a partner and later quarreled with the partner. In the worst of worlds, such squabbles can lead you into a courtroom, suing or being sued, paying lawyers, miserable and anxious.

Find out if the equity sharing partner has any history of litigation. If the seller has shared equity with other persons, phone those people and ask them if they are happy with the arrangement. Inquire into the reputation and financial stability of anyone with whom you are considering sharing property.

Home ownership is a highly emotional matter for

most people, and for most of us the home is our single greatest investment. If you do have a falling out with your equity partner, it can be a devastating and bitter experience. So go forth bravely, but cautiously!

Equity Sharing and Parents

Parents of adult children are ideal candidates for equity sharing, and often this is a way they can help their kids acquire a home by using their good credit for the mortgage and their savings for the down payment. Typically, the adult children live in the house and make the mortgage payments. In time, they can sell the house and split the profits, or buy out their parents' share, or perhaps inherit the parents' interest.

Equity Sharing and Taxes

The investor (parent, friend, or business associate) who puts up the down payment but does not live in the house can still get some hefty tax benefits from the equity sharing arrangement. The way it's done is that the nonresident partner officially rents his or her half of the house to the resident partner.

The rent is precisely equal to the nonresident's half of the mortgage payment plus taxes and insurance. That way, the nonresident can also claim depreciation deductions, under IRS Schedule E. "Depreciation" is an income tax deduction available to landlords to compensate for general decline and upkeep expenses in a home. As long as the landlord's annual adjusted gross income is $100,000 or less, he or she can deduct up to $25,000. Consult your tax adviser for the latest changes in IRS rules, but be sure to point out to your parents or co-buyer that these tax advantages are available.

Equity Sharing and Trouble

There is one significant danger for the nonresident investor, and that is the difficulty in getting rid of a resident investor if that person simply stops paying the mortgage. It's not as easy to evict a co-owner as it is a tenant. And if you, the resident co-owner lacking credit, should happen to declare bankruptcy, your creditors can attack your half interest in the property, which could be a real nightmare to the nonresident investor.

These are thorny, if unlikely, problems that reinforce our statement that you should be very careful to maintain an excellent rapport with your equity partner. Even parents and children can fight over property and never speak to each other again.

Don't enter into an equity share unless you really trust your partner, and don't do it without a legal written contract, as required by IRS Code 280A.

After all those scary warnings, however, we still think equity sharing is a perfect vehicle for some people without credit to get into home ownership.

CHAPTER NINE

Foreclosure to You

What a racket it is. In the early 1990s we've been observing the highest rate of foreclosure and default on real estate loans this nation has seen since the Great Depression. The sad truth is that high unemployment and diminished expectations have led a lot of honest people to the point where they can't keep up payments they agreed to, so in the end they lose their property in foreclosure.

Just as in the Depression, however, those individuals who have some cash on hand and/or good credit can now swoop in and buy those foreclosed and distressed properties at bargain basement rates. Professional investors attend the court foreclosure auctions with their pockets literally full of cash (or cashier's checks) and pick up good houses for a fraction of their former value.

This practice has given rise to a new kind of no-credit home purchase which we call "foreclosure to you." The professional buys the house, then turns around and sells it to the buyer with inadequate credit at a profit. The investor finances the purchase, so you don't have to qualify at a bank or mortgage company. In some cases, you don't need a down payment, just closing costs.

But you may pay a higher price for the house in such an arrangement, and you should be extra careful who you are dealing with. It's only reasonable to assume that people who make a specialty of buying houses in foreclosure auctions will not hesitate to foreclose on *you* as soon as possible if your payments fall behind.

Nonetheless, we encourage you to look into these deals, because they do provide a way to stop paying rent and get into home ownership without credit, and as long as you can meet the terms and have safe, legal title, something like this could be just what you need.

Mike F. and Steve P. are examples of professional investors who sell houses in this fashion in Phoenix, Arizona. Both of them run newspaper ads saying, "I sell houses. No qualifying. I'll finance. Phone xxx-xxxx." They don't actually have any listings. They take calls from prospective home buyers like yourself, talk to you about what kind of house you're looking for, which neighborhoods you're interested in, and how much you can afford. Then, they go out and try to find a house for you. Mike even says, "Find a house you like, and I'll buy it for you!"

They look for houses that are either in foreclosure proceedings or already foreclosed upon. The court is required to publish the addresses of property scheduled for foreclosure, and those lists are public knowledge, so you can drive around and inspect homes that are on the "endangered list." Up to the moment the foreclosure happens, you can still buy the house directly from the owner. Sometimes this is called a "race to the record," because many home purchases take place mere hours or minutes before the foreclosure is about to happen.

Once the foreclosure is final, however, the house may be put up for auction in the court, and anyone can bid on it. The only hitch is that the court will demand cash for the property. In other words, an investor with good credit can pick up a distressed property for a down payment and get a mortgage one way or other, but a foreclosed property sold at auction requires all cash on the barrel head.

In either case, however, the investor can turn around and sell the house to you, even if you have no credit.

Mike F. has adopted a new concept in financing—the 40-year home mortgage at a slightly above-average interest rate. He buys the home for you, the home you've agreed in advance that you want, then sells it to you for a down payment and monthly mortgage payment that guarantees him a good profit. The 40-year mortgage has a due-on-sale clause, meaning that you have to cash Mike out if you sell the place. Typically, he says, people sell within seven years. Few people would pay off a mortgage over 40 years, but if they did, they'd have paid for the house many times over. The profit is in the interest, of course.

Mike's a nice enough guy, but he's not in the business of being charitable to people who fall behind in their payments. You could say he fairly circles over-head like a vulture, waiting for his moment. "Look, I feel sorry for these people," he says, "but I didn't create their problems." And he didn't create your problems with credit, nor will he give you any kind of grace if you should lose your job or your health.

Foreclosure Scam Artists

Mike at least appears to be completely honest and legal. He's been in the business for many years, answers his own phone, and has great references. Not everyone in the foreclosure game is necessarily aboveboard, however. Buyer beware this kind of scam, which we have observed being practiced up and down the West Coast:

The ad in the paper says "Why pay rent? We buy foreclosure houses at auction and sell to you for nothing down, no credit required. Just call xxx-xxxx." You call and get a tape-recorded message that goes on for several minutes with a pitch that's just too good to be true. "Enroll in our program and we'll show you how to get rich in seven to eight years. We provide you with listings for over 500 foreclosure houses a month. Pick out the house you want, we'll buy it for you at auction, and sell it to you for nothing down, with no qualifying, no credit. But since you are paying nothing up front, the only thing we ask you to pay is the closing costs, typically $1,500. You don't need a job or credit references, but you must have $1,500 for the closing costs. Sound easy? It is! Leave us your name and phone number so we can invite you to our next free seminar, where we explain how our system works."

There are variations on this theme, but these outfits always have a clever-sounding name around the idea of quitting paying rent. "Landlord Busters," "Foreclosure Kings," "Rent No More." You can never reach a live individual on the phone; they must call you back. And they won't give you the details until you come to their "free informative seminar."

The catch, every time, is that they want you to pay the $1,500 (or $1,250 to $2,000) "closing costs" in advance. This is your fee for "enrolling" in their "program." And they assure you that the full amount will be applied to your closing costs when they buy you that foreclosure house at some time in the future. They are careful to state that they will *bid* on the house for you, but there is no guarantee their bid will be accepted.

We have no evidence that such schemes are illegal

or dishonest, but despite much investigation, we've yet to find a single person who actually bought a house using these programs. Our advice is *don't* ever hand over a fee for "closing costs" or anything else on a house you haven't bought or seen yet. And remember when they tell you about the 500 listings a month that foreclosure notices are public record. You can get the same lists without paying a cent. It's very easy for these fast-talking artists to string you along for months, telling you that the house you wanted was outbid. And it's easy for them to pack up and leave town after they've gotten enough people to "enroll" in their "program" and pay up front.

This is not just paranoia. Alas, there are crooks in the real estate business, as if you didn't know. Beware of anyone who is pushing "exclusive listings" that you have to pay for, whether for rentals or foreclosure sales or any other kind of real estate. No honest agent or broker charges money to look at listings. Some of these scam artists go from town to town, changing their names and the names of their businesses. These outfits can look completely legitimate, with nice furniture, well-dressed sales people, seminars held in major hotels. Beware if the company is so new that it's not listed in the phone book. Insist on references. Demand proof. Ask to meet in person at least three people who have bought a house through that agency, and ask to meet them in their houses. Most of all, don't pay in advance for anything until you are making a legitimate purchase offer on a specific house with an established escrow holder.

Having issued that warning, however, we still think foreclosure houses can be a wonderful opportunity to get a home without qualifying credit.

More Foreclosure Warnings

The foreclosure auction can be a frustrating experience. They are often postponed or canceled at the last minute, and you can do quite a lot of running around with little to show for it. Also, things can happen so fast at an auction that the property you want is gone before you have a chance to make a bid. There even are cases of people who mistakenly bid on the wrong house, and wind up owning something they didn't want.

If you're even considering buying a foreclosure house, you owe it to yourself to attend a few of these auctions and quietly observe what goes on. It's another case of the rich getting richer. If you happen to have the cash on hand, you might be able to pick up real estate at 80 percent or less of its appraised value.

But don't think that you can get a house for 50 percent of its value! The court will invariably establish a minimum bid, and that minimum price is a matter of public record. The foreclosure sharks attending the auction will carry a cashier's check already made out for the minimum amount, and an undetermined amount of cash to make up the difference if the successful bid is higher.

Another thing to consider with a foreclosed property is that it is always sold "as-is." That means if you later discover a serious flaw in the property, you have no recourse. You can inspect the property before you buy it, but sometimes even very serious problems are not obvious.

The final caveat here is emotional as well as financial. Ask yourself if you really want to buy a house that some other person has lost to foreclosure. The house has a history of failure, you might say. It would be helpful to know exactly why the previous owner was unable or unwilling to make the payments. Was it a personal tragedy such as illness, death in the family, sudden loss of job? Or was there something wrong with the house itself, or the neighborhood the house is in, which caused that homeowner to effectively give up?

Be very careful that somebody else's troubles don't become your own. It's not easy to get foreclosed upon. Most lenders will bend over backward to give the homeowner a chance to catch up on overdue payments. Long before foreclosure happens, the owner receives late-payment notices, warnings, letters, invitations to consult the credit counselor at the bank. Many mortgage lenders will accept a partial payment if the homeowner can't come up with the entire amount at one time. If nothing else, a homeowner can often sell the house (perhaps at a good profit) before being foreclosed upon. So why do people simply surrender their property?

It's an important question, and one you would be wise to ask before buying a foreclosed property. Some people become emotionally upset when they fall behind in their mortgage, so they lock the door and turn off the phone and just do nothing, as if that will help solve the problem. It doesn't. While the slow, laborious process of foreclosure is lumbering along, they could be selling their home and at least retrieving their investment in it, but instead they wait until it's too late.

Buying such a distressed property, one that is scheduled for foreclosure but not yet foreclosed on, can be a terrific boon for the person with inadequate credit, however. The seller in a case like that is truly desperate, and may be happy to sell the home to anyone who can bring the payments up to date and take over the assumable mortgage while giving him some cash for his equity.

The seller may even be willing to finance the sale in a wraparound mortgage, where he continues to be responsible for his mortgage and you pay him directly. If you make a deal like that, however, be sure to insist on monthly proof that the previous owner has made his payment on the first mortgage— a photocopy of a canceled check, or receipt from the mortgage holder. Any homeowner who got within shouting distance of foreclosure may fall into arrears again, so beware. The person may be an innocent, honest homeowner with bad luck, or there may be a culprit such as alcohol or drugs involved, or just plain senility. We've seen tragic incidents where helpless elderly people, unaware of the trouble they are in, lose their property in foreclosure even though they have money in the bank to pay the mortgage.

Remember that foreclosure is the most dire thing that can happen in real estate, and you need to be extra careful in buying foreclosed property.

Foreclosure Looms

We'd rather be in the business of dispensing happy tales, but foreclosure is never a happy event and there is usually a sad story behind it. Consider this ad: "Foreclosure looms. Hurry! Ocean view, 2 bdrm, 2 ba., possible assume FHA 7½. $115K Hurry for best deal. Phone xxx-xxxx after 5. By owner."

We called.

After years of buying houses and exposure to hundreds if not thousands of agents and sellers, it's easy to pick up the telltale signs of a desperate seller. The owner was eager to get rid of this property, to say the least. "I'm being driven out of town," he admitted candidly. "I haven't had any work for six months and can't find a job. They're on my case something bad."

"They" in this case invariably meant the banks, the collection agents, the powers of financial responsibility and foreclosure.

The "ocean view" turned out to be a distant one, indeed. The house was in southeast San Diego, in the most gang-infested and dangerous part of town, but located on a hill with a far-off view of the water. "The view would be better if I could ever get my neighbor to cut his tree," the seller said bitterly. Translation: bad neighborhood and unpleasant neighbor.

The assumable FHA loan at 7½ percent was for only $22,000. A second mortgage, also assumable without credit, was $68,000 and fixed at an amazing 17½ percent, with a large balloon cashout due in seven months' time. "I'm sure they'd be happy to let you assume the loan," the seller said. "They'll take anybody who will make the payment." The lender was a finance company that would gladly extend the term of the loan to any buyer willing to pay their sky-high interest rates.

Sorry to say, we expect this unfortunate seller to face the foreclosure rather than sell his home with the burden of that high-interest loan on top of the problems of his beleaguered neighborhood. His only hope or salvation lies in finding a buyer who's willing to pay 17½ percent interest in a time when qualified borrowers can get a mortgage under 9 percent, and even unqualified buyers can do a lot better. Or, he may sell for cash to a foreclosure specialist who turns it around and resells it at favorable rates.

A Final Word on Foreclosure

Put simply, you need to be extra careful in dealing with foreclosed or about-to-be-foreclosed properties. We strongly advise you to consult an attorney to check any documents, or at the very least work with a professional real estate broker. Foreclosure deals are not for the average home buyer. They are more complicated and can involve a tangled web of debts and claims (liens) against the property. Swim with these sharks at your own risk.

If you do find a foreclosure or other financially distressed house that you like, and it's available without credit, be absolutely certain that you receive clear, safe, and unclouded title at the close of escrow. A "clouded" title is one that is under dispute or subject to claims.

These deals are adventuresome, dangerous, and potentially very profitable.

CHAPTER TEN

Quitclaim

Nothing could be easier than quitclaiming as a method of acquiring property without credit. A quitclaim is simply a grant, whereby the co-owner of a house voluntarily signs over his or her interest to you, with or without payment. If you can find a person with good credit who is willing to buy a house with you, using his or her credit to qualify for the mortgage, then the person or persons can simply quitclaim the deed over to you and, voilà, you become the sole owner despite having no credit.

There's no real catch to this except the obvious fact that a mortgage lender is not going to let the original borrower off the hook just because he quitclaims to you. If the mortgage is based entirely on that person's credit, then he or she will remain liable in case you fail to make your payments. The bank or lender can go after the quitclaimer.

That doesn't really matter as long as there is a great deal of trust between the two parties, the buyer without credit and the person who allows his or credit to be used in this fashion—and as long as you make the payments on time. The lender will hold the original buyer responsible for the entire life of the mortgage, or until you sell the house and either pay off the mortgage or pass it on to the new buyer.

This kind of arrangement is most likely to happen within a family, but no blood relationship is necessary and some people are close enough friends to trust each other more than they trust their own relatives.

Doug Starr got his house in Joplin, Missouri, through a quitclaim from his grandfather. Doug was a young (25) landscape gardener lacking enough credit for a mortgage, whereas his grandad had plenty of credit and a good reputation in the community, and the two got along well. In fact, grandfather and grandson bypassed Doug's parents, whom neither of them got on with.

They bought the two-story farmhouse together with the old man's credit qualifying for the mortgage, and with the understanding that Doug would take care of his grandfather and eventually receive full title to the house as part of his inheritance. They lived together for five years, Grandad had a stroke and later died, but not before he quitclaimed his share of the property to Doug for $5. In the meantime, the house increased in value from about $40,000 in 1985 to $60,000 in 1990.

Doug was left with the deed to the house, the mortgage payment and, unfortunately, a hefty tax obligation, but he definitely benefitted from the gift. When he moved to Key West, Florida, to be a landscape artist for the rich, he rented out the house he and Grandad had bought to his own father, who had separated from his mother. The father paid the son a monthly rent to live in a house originally bought by the grandfather, then quitclaimed over. If the arrangement seems a bit unusual, it's perfectly legal and it worked out fine for everyone involved.

Of course, the bank can no longer go after Doug's grandfather in case of any default, because he's dead. They could foreclose on Doug if he quit making payments, but he's always paid on time and that payment record alone has given him excellent credit by now. He's getting tired of Florida and figures eventually he'll return to Missouri and move back into the house.

Andrew Malone didn't have such a gratifying experience with the duplex he bought with his mother in Manchester, New Hampshire. Everything was fine with Andrew and his wife and children living in one of the units, and his mother in the second, until the mother quitclaimed her interest not to Andrew but to her only daughter, his sister Bridget.

That left the mother liable for the credit, even though Andrew was (as always) paying the entire monthly mortgage amount, and his sister became his co-owner. Even so, nothing went wrong until the mother died, Bridget married a piano teacher from Boston, and brother and sister quarreled. Although she'd never lived there and only recently acquired an interest in the duplex, Bridget and her new hubby demanded their share of the property in cash, which Andrew couldn't possibly raise. He was forced to sell the duplex to meet his sister's demands, and saw his own family displaced from a home they had occupied and paid the mortgage on for more than ten years.

Andrew and Bridget never spoke to each other after that. He swore that he'd never again buy property in conjunction with another person, not even a close relative. When, years later, Andrew finally bought another home, his credit was good enough to buy a single-family house. His story illustrates the hazards of a quitclaim arrangement, and the immense bitterness between family members that can result. It's not unusual for loved ones to part forever after fighting over real estate. Even when Andrew died and Bridget attended his funeral, Andrew's wife, Helene, refused to speak to her sister-in-law. These two ladies sat for three days on opposite sides of the open casket containing Andrew's body. "I can't prevent her from being here," said Helene, "but after she took our house away, why should I have anything to do with her?"

And that's not even the worst-case scenario. Imagine the chagrin of landlady Sylvia Moss of Pueblo, Colorado, who liked her tenant Jim Babcock so much that she agreed to put up her substantial credit as a co-signer when Jim fell into a bargain deal on a great little bungalow. She quitclaimed her share over to Jim, as they had agreed in advance, but was dismayed when only six months later Jim couldn't keep up his mortgage payments and the bank went straight to Sylvia for relief. In fact, they gave up trying to collect from Jim even though he lived in the house because he was out of work and Sylvia had more assets. Soon she was deluged with calls from collection agents. The friendship between former landlady and tenant became very strained.

Sylvia made a few payments to get Jim back out of debt, and began nagging him to sell the bungalow if he couldn't pay his own mortgage. Because they were such good friends, Jim didn't want Sylvia to suffer, so he eventually sold the house and (you guessed it) went back to renting from Sylvia. The taste of home ownership has him addicted, however, and he's actively looking around for another house he can buy without credit and without Sylvia's partnership.

It is theoretically possible that someone who quitclaims property to another person could wind up paying for the property for years, in order to avoid besmirching their credit rating, while the smug creditless person sits in the house, legally owning something he hasn't paid for. It is possible, but we haven't found a single case of such a dire thing happening. Perhaps that's because the only person who would cosign for a mortgage and then quitclaim the property to someone lacking credit would be a very close relative or friend, someone in a relationship of absolute trust.

If you have such a person in your life, a relative or friend who is willing to trust you with a house mortgage, be glad! Don't hesitate to use that trust and love to feather your nest. You're one of the lucky ones.

It's worth adding that the person with good credit doesn't necessarily have to quitclaim the property to you, the buyer without credit. In some cases, people simply buy property together and hold it together, as an equity sharing arrangement. One party has credit, the other doesn't. The banks don't care how bad your credit is as long as your partner's is excellent and that person is willing to take full responsibility in case you flake out and miss payments.

The quitclaim action can happen the day after you buy the house, or any number of years later. In the case of a parent and child buying together, you may simply inherit the other person's equity as joint tenants with the right of survivorship. More about inheritance and buying from the elderly follows in the next chapter.

CHAPTER ELEVEN

En Viager, Buying From the Old, Dying, and Dead

You can't take it with you, according to the eternal verity, and so one way or another people who die have to pass along their real estate to another person or entity. We don't mean to be facetious. Obtaining property from the elderly or the deceased isn't limited to inheritance.

The French have a system called "en viager," which allows a homeowner over the age of 65 to sell the home while living there the rest of his or her life. In the United States, we have the life estate grant, similar to "en viager" in that the property changes hands but the elderly person retains a lifetime right to occupancy.

Reverse mortgages, estate liquidation sales to settle probate and emergency sales to pay estate taxes, are other ways that people without credit can and do buy real estate from the old, terminally ill, or dead.

Let's examine this French "en viager" system for a moment. We don't conventionally sell real estate in this fashion in the United States, but there's absolutely no laws against it, and with some modification the same plan could work perfectly well in this country.

First of all, the seller must be 65 or older and will get the right to remain in the house until death, so the buyer is taking a gamble on the health of the seller. The seller will sometimes feign a terrible illness, moaning and groaning and acting as if he or she is only steps away from the grave. Then, the moment the sale is legal and complete, a sudden vigor returns!

The buyer pays the old person a down payment on the house, called a "bouquet," and agrees to pay a certain amount every month. When the seller dies, the buyer acquires the house, with no further obligation to the seller's estate. If the seller owned the place free and clear, the buyer gets the property with no further payments of any kind.

The bizarre part of this, from an American point of view, is that there is no fixed price for the house. It all depends on how long the elderly person lives. If the seller dies soon, the buyer gets a terrific bargain. On the other hand, if the seller hangs on to the age of 110, the buyer could possibly pay two or three times the value of the house!

Another thing: If the buyer misses even one monthly payment, every penny (or franc) he or she has paid into the house is forfeited. Talk about motivation for getting your check in the mail! Some would say this arrangement could even be motivation for murder.

Buying real estate "en viager" is illegal in neighboring Switzerland. Not here, however.

Clearly, this system works best with a seller who has no children or heirs, and who owns the house free and clear, with the mortgage paid off.

Applying the same principle to this country, we've come up with the concept of the reverse mortgage, which has become increasingly popular. Reverse mortgage finance companies will buy a home from an elderly person, pay that seller a monthly amount, and take title to the property when the person either dies or moves out. The only real difference between reverse mortgages and "en viager" is that a definite price is established on the house. When the old person dies, the reverse mortgage company still must pay off the difference owed on the house to the seller's heirs or estate. The seller is guaranteed a monthly check for life, however, so it's possible the company could pay more than the house is worth if the owner lives a long time. These companies work from insurance statistics with fairly reliable predictions of how long a person will live. The amount they pay every month depends on how old the seller or sellers are, and how much the house is deemed to be worth.

There's no reason why an individual buyer couldn't essentially issue a reverse mortgage to an elderly seller. Many old people are house-rich but cash-poor. They've worked hard all their lives, paid off a mortgage, and watched their house increase in value perhaps 20 or 30 times over. They're sitting on a gold mine but living on chicken feed. A reverse mortgage allows them to get extra money every month and substantially improve the quality of their lives, without having to leave their home. And that can be a great deal for both the pensioner and the struggling buyer without credit, because the vast majority of older homeowners want nothing more than to stay in their homes until they die, comfortable and safe and with an income that protects their dignity.

Life Estate Grants

Many older homeowners essentially give their property to their children, but retain a lifetime use of the place. This is a simple life estate grant, and the purpose is to avoid probate. When the parent dies, the inheriting child is already the legal owner of the house and doesn't need to pay taxes or get involved in complicated procedures for taking title.

The personal reverse mortgage we suggested earlier is nothing more than a life estate grant in which you as the buyer are paying for the property rather than getting it for nothing.

By the way, a life estate grant always includes a clause that requires the homeowner to keep the property in good repair and pay the taxes. If your elderly parent or seller gets Alzheimer's disease or just becomes cranky and uncooperative and lets the house go to shambles, you as holder of the life estate grant have a legal right to enter the premises, make the repairs, and otherwise protect your property. It really *is* your property already, even though you can't have it until the old person passes on.

If you have a close friend who is getting along in years, has no children or heirs, and owns a home outright, you're only a breath away from making a deal that will eventually get you a home without needing credit. There are also times when people make an agreement to take care of an older person, be a nurse and companion, in exchange for eventually inheriting the property. All such arrangements, reverse mortgages and life estate grants *must* be in writing and legally binding. This is one area in which we strongly recommend you employ a competent attorney to draw up the papers.

There are many unfortunate things that can happen to an elderly homeowner, of course. What if the person's health deteriorates so much that he or she must go into a nursing home? With most life estate grants, the seller retains a right to the home even in that circumstance. The reasoning here is that perhaps the health will improve, and the elderly person should have the right to go back to the home. It's a very humane arrangement, all things considered, and it need not be exploitative. By purchasing a home from an elderly person, you could be that person's angel and best friend.

Everybody knows some senior citizen who lives alone in an older home. It's a sad commentary on our society that families don't keep their elders together with the younger generations.

Buying from the Departed

Not to be morbid, but if you can buy a house from a terminally ill person, you can certainly also buy one from a deceased person. All kinds of things can happen to their real property when someone dies, even if there are heirs. Look for estate liquidation sales (probate) and emergency sales to pay estate taxes, and you may find property that you can buy without needing credit simply because the sellers have an urgent need to get rid of it.

A classic example is a house we bought from the estate of Minnie Skinner in Seattle. She had died in the house after going blind there, stringing nylon stocking ropes all over the place at waist level to guide her through the rooms. The only heir was a distant nephew who had no use for the house and wanted only to sell it as soon as possible to settle Minnie's probate, taxes, and estate. The nephew hired a lawyer who sold the house to us for nothing down, with no credit, and the promise of a deferred down payment to be made in a year's time.

The place was a wreck, but in less than a year we had fixed it up and sold it for a tidy profit—even before the down payment came due. The nephew got his cash out of it, and we went on down the road, looking for the next deal.

So be sure to read the obits. Become a volunteer at the local senior citizens' center. Be an advocate for the elderly and you could buy yourself a great home without credit.

Of course, you cannot legally or ethically take advantage of an elderly person who is lacking in mental competence. We can't state this too emphatically. There are unscrupulous individuals who do just that, but their actions are reprehensible.

If the elderly person is declared mentally incompetent by a court or public authority, he or she doesn't have the legal right to transfer title to you or engage in a sale transaction. But even if the person has not been formally declared incompetent, if you take advantage of someone who's senile or incapable of handling his or her own affairs, that person's heirs or the district attorney can later sue you to retrieve the property, which is legally stolen.

In an ideal situation, the elderly seller will have some professional advice or an advocate or representative not related or obligated to you, the buyer. And in all cases, your legal papers and transfers must be proper and airtight.

You cannot "take" property from the elderly, but you can buy it without credit under the right circumstances and benefit the older person and yourself as well.

CHAPTER TWELVE

The Unwanted, the Desperate, and the Ugly

As the chapter title suggests, you have a far better chance of buying a house without credit if the house itself is what we politely term "property in trouble." That doesn't mean it isn't a good house, worth owning, but only that for one reason or other it's difficult to sell. Therefore, the owner may be willing to sell it to an unqualified buyer, or indeed any buyer.

There are a thousand good reasons why somebody might need to sell a house, reasons that don't affect the value of the house itself. Divorce, death, bankruptcy, job transfer, illness, or imprisonment are all examples of bad things that can happen to good people, who then *must* sell their home.

But this chapter looks at the house itself and pinpoints areas in which the problems with the real estate may make it possible for you to buy without credit. Just be sure that whatever is wrong with the house is something you can fix, tolerate, live with, or otherwise accept!

1. Location, location, location. This is the oldest axiom in real estate. The location of the home is probably more important than the home itself, because you can't change where it is no matter how much you might improve the house. And a bad, or less than desirable, location can make a house very difficult to sell. A few examples:

• **Directly in front of or next to a school.** Even parents with school-age children don't necessarily want to live near a school. Kids are loud, and nothing is noisier than hundreds of them en masse, arriving in the morning and leaving in the afternoon and hanging around the playground or schoolyard. In some inner cities, schools can also attract drug dealers, gangs, petty violence, and theft. Oddly enough, however, not everybody hates living near a school. We find that retired people, grandparents, sometimes enjoy locating near an elementary school simply because they absolutely love small children.

• **In a dangerous, crime-infested neighborhood.** Few things will reduce the value of a home more than a vicinity known for its crime rate. If you can put up with security locks on your door, vandalism of your car, constant vigilance, and apprehension, you can sometimes get a wonderful house without credit that would cost twice as much in a better neighborhood. Banks are not legally allowed to "red-line" certain neighborhoods, excluding them from loans, but the reality is that a mortgage lender will be reluctant to invest in a bad location. That reality might tend to force the seller to offer financing without qualifying credit.

• **In an area with a depressed economy and high unemployment.** Seattle in the 1970s, Dallas in the 1980s, Phoenix in the 1990s, are examples of cities where slumping local economies drove down the prices of homes. When there are no jobs available in a town, you'll find vacant homes abandoned by owners who were forced to move on, looking for work. If you're one of the lucky people with a stable job, or you're self-employed, a weak economy can actually help you buy without credit. When the economy rebounds and new jobs open, your house may increase tremendously in value.

• **At a great distance from civilization.** Sometimes rural property is a lot cheaper and easier to buy than urban, convenient real estate, unless the rural area happens to be a prosperous resort. If you're willing to live way out in the middle of nowhere, commuting a long way to your job or working at home, you'll get a lot more house for less money. Some farming communities in the Midwest have become virtual ghost towns.

• **In a place with bad weather.** You can't really overstate the importance of climate to real estate values. If the house is located in a town that gets brutally hot (like certain parts of Florida and the California desert) or unbearably cold (northern Maine, North Dakota) or is subject to windstorms, tornados, floods, any kind of severe weather, you might find a homeowner who will do anything to move on. Make sure the weather is something you're willing to tolerate! There are rare individuals who claim to thrive on 120-degree heat or 30-below zero cold. Of course, extreme weather will drive up your utility bills for heating or air-conditioning, too.

• **In a noisy neighborhood.** Most of us don't want to live in a place that's roaring with noise. Just recently, we saw a beautiful Victorian home in San Diego go for $11,000 down and $1,000 a month with no qualifying credit. The house was in excellent condition, with a large yard, but it was located right next door to a 24-hour gas station on a busy, congested intersection with four lanes of incessant traffic. Not a peaceful location, but the proud new owners plan to construct a brick wall around the property borders!

• **Near an airport.**   We've seen houses advertised as "convenient to the airport," which is just about the worst thing a house can be! Before buying a home in the vicinity of an airfield, be sure to go there and test the decibel level of airplane noise at all times of day and night.

• **In any area scheduled for major construction or road building.**   Ask the agent and the seller and doublecheck if you have any suspicion that a major highway or other big construction project is scheduled in the neighborhood. Sometimes, good houses are virtually given away because the neighborhood is about to become intolerable. And the seller is not necessarily obliged by law to disclose it, so beware.

• **With objectionable neighbors.**   You'd better believe that the neighbors affect the value and salability of a home, and you'd better find out everything you can about them before you buy. If the house next door looks seedy, with all kinds of debris and junk salvage strewn around the yard, consider what kinds of people live there. If they keep a vicious dog on a chain, barking all night, how are you going to get your sleep? More than just the immediate next-door neighbors, consider the demographics of the entire neighborhood. We have seen some wonderful homes that were hard to sell because of the neighbors, but somebody else's bad relationships don't necessarily carry over to you.

Those are a few location problems. No doubt you can imagine others. Let's go on to other problems of the desperate, the unwanted, and the ugly.

2. The price. Sometimes a house is difficult to sell simply because the owner is asking too much for it, and refuses to come down on the price. If you're willing to pay a bit more, you might be able to swing a deal without credit. All real estate agents will give you "comparables," prices that nearby homes with similar features sold for within the last six months. A bank may refuse to finance a mortgage for more than 80 percent of appraised value. But a smart seller can sometimes get a higher price if he or she is willing to offer creative financing without credit approval. And you may be willing to pay a higher amount for the convenience of such financing.

3. The utilities. If the house has very high utility bills, it may be harder to sell and therefore available without credit. Check into this carefully. Before buying any home, ask to see the past three months' utility bills. A house that costs a fortune to heat in the winter or cool in the summer can really tear into your budget. Remember, however, that some utility bill problems can be corrected. The house may need to be reinsulated, rewired, or change over to another form of heat. You might be able to cut the water bill in half if you install slow-flow faucets and drip irrigation, and such. If you do find high utility costs, by all means use that as an argument to lower the price of the home or talk the owner into easier credit terms.

4. The owner has moved. When a house is vacant and the seller has moved, he is doubly motivated to sell because he's probably paying his old mortgage as well as the costs of his new place to live. That can become a tremendous burden, so that the seller becomes desperate for someone, anyone, to move into the house and relieve him of the payments. Nothing

is worse for a house than sitting empty, because of
the risk of vandalism as well as general, slow disin-
tegration. But nothing is better for a buyer lacking
credit than an empty house that's been on the market for six months or more! Such a house is an ideal
candidate for owner financing, lease option, equity
sharing, or even adverse possession.

Conventional real estate thinking is that the best
way to sell a house is when it's furnished, occupied,
and looks its best. Our advice is to hunt for exactly
the opposite: a house that's empty and looks its
worst. It's helpful to know exactly why the owner
moved, but there's no guarantee he'll tell you the
truth. There are endless legitimate reasons for moving that don't diminish the value of the house, however. It also may be possible for you to do a more
thorough investigation of the condition of the property simply because it's empty.

Find a house that's been empty for six months,
and you're very likely to find a motivated seller.

5. The property is in bad condition. This is an
obvious problem that could lead to your being able
to buy a house without credit. You have to decide
for yourself just how bad a condition you're willing
to accept, however. If the house has serious structural problems, such as a cracked foundation or
falling-down roof, you'd be well advised to get guaranteed professional estimates on the cost of the repairs before making an offer to buy. Call in a
legitimate contractor, plumber, electrician, or
whomever and ask them to give you a quote in writing and guarantee the price for at least six months.
Don't take on a home repair job that's way above
your financial capability.

Some bad conditions are repairable with merely
cosmetic work, things like paint, wallpaper, floor

tiles, carpets, and so forth. Other conditions can be wildly expensive to repair—faulty plumbing, termite rot, inadequate wiring, defective septic system, broken furnace, to name a few. If you're looking at a home that's in visibly bad shape, it's worth paying a professional home inspector for a thorough report.

Once you've determined precisely how much it will cost to bring the house into good repair, present those figures to the seller as an argument to reduce either the price or the terms. A house that can't pass inspection also can't qualify for an FHA mortgage or bank mortgage, so the seller may be forced to offer financing without qualifying credit.

6. The floor plan is awkward. A bad floor plan can be a serious flaw in a house, and make it difficult to sell. It's hard to understand why some houses are built with ridiculously awkward interior arrangements, such as a bedroom that can be reached only by walking through a bathroom, or a laundry room inconveniently located in the cellar. Variations are endless. A good floor plan separates the living room in a dead-end location, so that you don't have to walk through it to get anywhere else in the house. A foyer or exterior porch is helpful for receiving guests and removing outer clothing in winter. The kitchen should have a separate entrance from the outside, so kids and pets can go in and out without tracking dirt and debris all over the living-room rug. A house has traffic patterns, with the heaviest use being in the kitchen and main bathroom. A lousy floor plan can make you miserable, but it also might make the house undesirable enough to be available without credit.

7. The mortgage is problematical. Some older homes were mortgaged in the days of 17 percent interest, and are stuck with a high payment. You would need to refinance the property, but that's not possible because you don't have the credit to qualify for a new loan. Sometimes the mortgage is an adjustable rate loan, giving you no assurance of how high the monthly payment could rise in inflationary times.

8. The builder went bankrupt, or disappeared. This problem relates to newer homes thrown up in the 1970s and 1980s by incompetent or corrupt builders and contractors who later go out of business or just vanish. It's a shocking national scandal. You've heard people say, "They just don't build houses like they used to," but that's not necessarily true. Some new homes are well constructed of sturdy materials. But some prefabricated homes are just plain poorly made, and start falling apart even while they are relatively young. Watch out for small things like doors that don't close snugly, dampness on the basement floor, cracks in the plaster. If you're looking at a home in a development of newer houses, by all means canvass the neighbors and ask them if they've had any problems with poor construction.

9. The house has a defect that makes it unbankable. This final flaw in our list will vary from state to state and bank to bank. Certain specific defects in a house will effectively prohibit a bank from issuing a mortgage, thus forcing the seller to provide alternative financing. In some places, the banks will not mortgage a house that lacks a foundation, even though you can live quite comfortably in a house without a foundation in the warmer parts of the Sunbelt states. Sometimes, the house is unbankable because it's had earthquake damage or sits too low in a floodplain and is subject to annual flooding, or has irreversible termite damage. The point here is simply that if you find you can tolerate or repair the defect, you can often buy such a house without needing credit.

So, dear home buyer, go out there and hang out with the desperate, the unwanted, and the ugly. Somebody else's problem could be your financial salvation and your dream home!

CHAPTER THIRTEEN

Go for It!

If you've read this far, you realize that there are many perfectly legitimate ways you can buy a home without needing any credit or bank approval. We've looked at the FHA and VA government assumable mortgages with no qualifying required; owner financing; lease options; 30 percent down payment financing; adverse possession; equity sharing; foreclosure sales; quitclaims; buying from the elderly and deceased; buying unwanted or distressed property.

Now let's really talk.

This kind of home buying is not for the faint of heart.

Anybody with a large down payment in cash and a terrific credit rating can walk into a bank and get a mortgage, assuming the house itself is up to standards. But those of us lacking the down payment or the credit, or both, have to be a lot more creative, aggressive, faithful, determined, persevering, persuasive, open-minded, and willing to take a risk.

These qualities may in fact describe the essence of a person or persons who can go out and buy a home despite lacking credit.

Here are some important guidelines to remember:

• **Be realistic.** Figure out what you really, absolutely can afford to pay every month, and find a home that costs no more. You're not doing yourself any favors if you get into a home purchase that's over your head and will cause you to fall behind in the payments. Include all the "hidden expenses" like closing costs, "points," taxes, insurance, and utilities.

Be realistic also about how much of a home you can get. Don't torture yourself longing for a mansion, a spiral staircase, or the ritziest neighborhood in town if you can't afford those things. It's just common sense that the nicer and more expensive the house is, the more a seller is going to worry about your credit. Remember that you can start with a smaller, less expensive home and build up your credit rating tremendously simply by paying your mortgage every month; every few years, with luck and work, you may be able to trade up to a better house, until that mansion is eventually yours.

• **Be flexible.** This is very important. If the house you want isn't available without credit, don't mourn. Find another house. If the terms you offer don't work, or the seller is not convinced, write another offer, change the terms, try another route. If the real estate agent is an unimaginative, nay-saying, discouraging, "you-can't-possibly-afford-to-buy-a-house" type, find another agent. A flexible agent with some imagination could be your biggest asset.

The exact deal you seek may not be possible. You may have to beg your old Uncle Pete for a loan, or sell your recreational vehicle to raise the money for the down payment. You might have to rent out a spare bedroom to meet the mortgage. Maybe you need to find an equity share because you simply can't afford to own a whole house on your own. Keep an open mind. Try everything. Examine all possibilities.

• **Don't give up.** No advice we can give is more important than this. Perseverance furthers. Trying to buy a home without credit can be a discouraging process, and you could be turned down again and again. If you give up too easily, you'll just be a renter all your life.

Buying a house is a mental game as well as a physical purchase. Take the attitude that if you don't get the house, it was not the right house for you! Another, better house is waiting for you somewhere. The right house is the one that's easy for you to buy. If you don't succeed with the house you are pursuing, pick yourself up, dust yourself off, and go after something else.

You could hit it lucky and find your dream home on the first Sunday that you go out looking around. But that's unlikely and perhaps not even desirable. Most people have to shop around and see at least 50 houses before finding the right deal. If that takes months or even years, don't despair. Don't give up!

• **Be honest.** Don't waste your own and the agents' and sellers' time looking at houses you can't possibly get on no-credit terms. Tell everyone up front what your situation is, and what you need: how much, if anything, you can come up with as a down payment; how much you can pay every month; how bad your credit, if any, really is. Get to the bottom line and adhere to it. Tell the truth and you have nothing to fear. Lie and exaggerate and waffle, and you could get into serious trouble. If you are honest, you are going to look only at houses that have some real chance of selling to a buyer without credit.

• **Put it in writing.** There comes a time when all the talk amounts to nothing unless you make your offer in writing. Especially when you are trying to convince a seller to sell you the house without credit, you should be able to demonstrate in writing the profit that seller will receive. Most homeowners don't realize all the options.

The typical seller has established a sale price for the house, and fantasizes that amount. "My house is worth $125,000 and my old mortgage is only $50,000, so I'm going to get $75,000 when I sell the place!" is conventional thinking. If, however, that same seller is willing to carry the paper (owner financing), he or she could actually receive double or triple the profit over a period of time! Prove it. Put it down on paper.

A savvy real estate agent will admit that if you write up an offer, *any* offer, you can never tell what will happen. We know buyers who offered way below the asking price of a house, sure that their offer would be refused, only to have it accepted. One thing for sure is that you can't succeed if you don't make an offer in writing.

• **Get your credit report.** The major credit agencies are required by law to let you see a copy of your own credit report. If you have been turned down for credit, they must send you a copy free of charge; otherwise, they charge a small service fee. The reason we make this suggestion is that you may find errors on your credit report, things that you can have changed which may improve your standing. Old bills that you've already paid may still be showing up on your credit report. The IRS is notorious for failing to remove liens that have been fully paid off. It could be that your credit is not as bad as you think it is. Even if it's absolutely terrible, it won't hurt you to know exactly what debts they are holding against you. Remember that debts more than seven years old (except for debts to the federal government) should be erased from your report under the statute of limitations laws.

• **Be brave.** "Faint heart ne'er won fair lady," or fine house. Buying a home can be scary and takes courage because for most of us the home purchase is the single greatest investment we make in our lives. Of course you have to be careful, but you can't be timid or too conservative.

Our wise banker friend, Lynne Ballew, refers to the whole of banking as "risk management," and home buying is similar. There's always a risk involved, and you can't win or even play the game without taking risks. Will the house appreciate in value, will it be worth more than you paid for it in a few years' time, or will the market go down? How about interest rates, will they go up or down? Will your business succeed, will you get promoted on your job? Take a chance, but not a foolish one. If you doubt that you know enough to take the risk, seek advice from someone whose real estate knowledge you respect. Don't be afraid, or you'll never get anywhere.

• **Do it now.** There's never been a better time. At this writing, two years into the 1990s, the whole nation is a buyer's market. Interest rates are low, bargains are everywhere (well, maybe not in Palm Beach, but who knows?), sellers are eager, and deals are there for the making. Don't hesitate to get started. Read the classified ads under homes and condos for sale, go to open houses on weekends, start making some phone calls, get out there and have a ball.

• **Let us know.** When you buy your house without credit, drop us a line in care of this publisher.

We are collecting stories of no-credit transfers and would love to hear your story and possibly include it in a later edition of this book. We care. We want you to succeed.

CHAPTER FOURTEEN:

Credit-Free and Home for the Holidays

Tales from the Depression

"Owner walk away. Take over payments, pay closing costs, give owner $2,000 and it's yours! Open House Sunday, 1-4, xxxx Mountain View Dr. Agt. 555-5555."

The ad was too fetching to resist, especially since the address on Mountain View Dr. was in a charming neighborhood of San Diego called Normal Heights. Why would anybody "walk away" from a house on that street? we wondered. Perhaps the place was in terribly dilapidated condition. We certainly hoped so!

"Unfortunately," however, it was in fine condition. It was a cute little house with a living room designed around a bar, which had a window view of the backyard deck and gardens. Two bedrooms, one bath, fully remodeled, two-car garage, fenced yard, great street, middle-class neighborhood, good freeway access. The price was $165,000, of which the seller owed a mortgage balance of $161,000.

That's no profit at all for the seller. In fact, by the time he pays the agent's commission, it's a loss. So why would he "walk away?" Greg, the agent, claimed the house was owned by two guys in an equity and domestic partnership. One was moving to Oregon, the other couldn't afford the place by himself. A likely story. But how could they have a $161,000 mortgage if that's all the house was worth?

Turns out the sellers had refinanced their loan in the heady, dizzying days of 1989–1990, before the big real estate crash hit San Diego. They had managed to convince a bank the place was worth $190,000, hence the size of their loan. But by late 1991, they couldn't find anyone willing to pay $165,000 for the house when equally good ones were going off at $160, $155, $150, and headed down.

Anybody with $2,000 and the closing costs could take over their payments in a wraparound mortgage, essentially seller financing, and own a rather nice house in a prestigious area. But nobody took them up on it. At this writing, the house is still available after six months on the market without a nibble.

It's only one of many houses available under such terms, houses offered for sale by owners who simply need to be relieved of the burden of their mortgage payments. These owners harbor no fantasy of getting rich or even getting back their investment from a house. They simply can't afford to own a home they have already bought and lived in, sometimes for years.

You can snap up one of these deals, but be careful. The amount of the underlying mortgage should not exceed 80 percent of the true, bare-bones, lowest-possible value of the house.

The house at $165,000 was too expensive for us. It was too perfect already, too remodeled, too in hock. We needed a fixer-upper for $125,000 or less, available without credit, and we asked Greg to look around for us. He promised he would and in fact started calling the next day with bargains galore.

Each One a Gem

The Spanish-style charmer on 32nd Street in Normal Heights was asking $128,900 (but would take less), and really had a great deal of style. The walls were sculpted, the doorways arched and coved. There was a wonderful living room with big fireplace, red tile roof, large covered deck, and fenced backyard.

The place was occupied, however. Eeek—tenants. Everybody knows tenants can be fiendishly difficult to get rid of, no matter how cooperative they may seem at first. It's not really in a tenant's interest to show the house to buyers, because the sale of the home is likely to force him to move, which he may not want or can't afford to do. In the worst-case scenario, the tenants stop paying rent and trash the house, forcing the owner to endure the lengthy and expensive process of eviction.

These particular tenants, a father and son, were said to be personal friends of the owner and able to move "on a moment's notice." Surrrre. The guy had a whole recording studio industry set up in the dining room, with tape-duplicating machines everywhere, and every room of the house was literally crammed with the tenants' possessions. Nonetheless, the agent said, there would be "no problem" in their moving out.

Don't believe everything an agent tells you, because some lies are "actionable" and amount to misrepresentation, whereas other lies are wrong and misleading but not illegal. How did this agent know "for sure" that those tenants would move quickly? She didn't, of course. The agent who sold us the house in Morongo Valley said the town had "plenty of water," true as far as it goes, but he neglected to mention that the water rate is among the highest in the U.S.A.! Our water bill for a single-family home was easily double or triple the norm in California.

We were about to make an offer on the Spanish charmer when I noticed the most peculiar thing: a mailbox posted on the backyard fence, and near it a creaky gate that led into the neighbor's backyard. The agent swore she didn't know anything about the oddly placed mailbox. The house itself got its mail delivered on the front porch.

It took several days to track down the information, but it finally turned out that the house in back actually received its mail in "our" house's backyard, and owned a permanent easement to enter there and collect it. In fact, the back house had a perpetual easement to walk right through "our" yard, and the postal carrier used that easement daily.

That's not all. The garage on "our" lot had been declared to be sitting on the property of the house in back, following a bitter litigation. The Spanish charmer house was allowed to keep and maintain the garage as-is, but could never renovate or change it without giving the land back to its rightful owner. "We" owned the garage, but "they" owned the land under it. It was an encroachment.

We didn't buy the Spanish charmer with its easement and encroachment. Neither did anyone else. The tenants are glad.

"Minnie Skinner's place" was billed as an "organic gardener's delight." The yard was loaded with fruit-bearing trees and vegetable gardens. The house was old, very small (600 square feet), with a weird floor plan that forced you to walk through one bedroom to get to the second bedroom. But it had a pleasant fireplace, was located on a quiet street of single-family homes, and had that fabulous organic garden. The price was $125,000, and the seller was an elderly lady who had already moved and owned the place free and clear.

Her name wasn't really "Minnie Skinner," but we called her that because she reminded us of another elderly lady, deceased, from whom Ray bought a house in Seattle (see chapter 11). This new Minnie Skinner had lived many years in the old house and tended the large garden, but claimed she had moved because she got too old and tired to do all the yard work. She bought another house with lower maintenance needs.

This place had some funky qualities that were classic warning signs. How good is the roof? we asked. "It's an old roof," she replied, "but it wasn't leaking the last time I lived here." The floors were sloping, but "all the old houses have that." The concrete driveway and slab in the backyard were cracked and broken.

She was clearly selling the backyard, not the house. If the whole thing was worth $125,000, at least a hundred grand of that was in avocados, lemons, oranges, and kumquats. The lot was oversized, with plenty of room to add on to the house, and fenced for privacy.

We figured this organic find was "ripe" for seller financing or a lease option, but Minnie flatly refused. She had bought her new home on a private real estate contract herself, and had promised the seller she would cash him out from the sale of her old house with garden. If she extended financing, she might not get her cash for years. If she even granted a lease option, she could tie up the money for a year. She just couldn't do it.

She also couldn't sell the house, not yet anyway, but for six months she's been sitting there every Saturday and Sunday afternoon with an Open House sign on the door, welcoming visitors to her garden of Eden. If she'd taken a year's lease option, she'd have the option fee plus six months of rent in her pocket and be within six months of closing escrow. As it is, she's received nothing but fruits and vegetables.

The Bancroft place, you wouldn't give a plug nickel for. It's an excellent example of how people can take a decent house in a reasonably tolerable neighborhood and turn it into a living nightmare nobody wants to inherit, even for nothing down with no credit required.

The Bancrofts had a noble Victorian house with hardwood floors, a fireplace, two generous sized bedrooms and a remodeled bathroom, plus garage and fenced-in backyard. Sounds good, right? And it was, basically, a solid house, but it had been trashed. The stove and refrigerator were gone. Rusty old appliances filled the yard. Someone had smashed a fist through a bedroom door ("Oh, the seller was so unhappy about leaving here, she punched the door," the agent said). Now we've heard everything. The windows were broken and taped up. The owners had not bothered to clean up after their dogs. They had started to build in kitchen cabinets but for some reason stopped midway through the project, building just enough to block access to the vent where the gas range was supposed to go. On and on. The place was a shambles, vacant, owners fled to another state.

The price of $127,000 was just about what they owed on their mortgage, which was delinquent and already in foreclosure proceedings.

This house is a bargain in the future. It's in such terrible condition that the lender will find it impossible to sell at the full mortgage value after foreclosure. Several investors are already waiting in the wings for that foreclosure and the auction that will follow. The bank or mortgage company is just going to take a bath on this one, and the Bancrofts will see their credit rating destroyed for six or seven years.

But somebody else will get lucky.

And the Bancrofts, wherever they are, can always buy another house, without credit of course!

Now here's a deal we couldn't believe, but it was real. The ad read "Lease option. No credit. Two-bedroom, two-bath condo with security parking, pool, spa, view." The owner was a single lady of 60 years who had lived there herself and wanted to sell the condo for retirement income, but not for four more years. So she offered it on a four-year lease with a purchase option at the end.

The way it worked was that the buyer would put down $1,600 to move in, then pay $800 a month for the first year, $100 of which applied toward the purchase. Every year, the rent went up a bit (to $835 the second year, $865 the third, and $900 the fourth) as the value of the condo was supposedly going to increase. At the end of four years, buyer and seller would negotiate the price of the condo based on an appraisal, so there was no actual fixed price on the unit.

That arrangement struck us as odd, and potentially even dangerous. What if the seller or buyer didn't agree with the appraisal after four years? Who gets to set the price? And what if the value of the condo goes down in that time? That's always possible.

Anyway, we went to see this wonder and found it was located in a complex of 65 apartments at the end of a cul-de-sac overlooking Fletcher Parkway, one of the smoggiest and busiest avenues in La Mesa, a suburb of San Diego. The "view" mentioned in the ad was a view of that roaring boulevard and a huge Mobil gas station that was directly below the building.

There was indeed a small pool and a spa capable of holding four people, which in a complex of 65 apartments isn't much. As we entered the courtyard, a flock of veiled women in long gowns came streaming out of several condos, wailing and shrieking at their barefoot children. The agent said he was required to show us the homeowners' association report, which mentioned severe earthquake damage in the north wing, three days of total evacuation of people and pets required for fumigation, and a spate of car thefts and burglaries in the complex. All of these problems, the report promised, would be corrected in the future.

The upstairs neighbor had allowed his bathtub to overflow to the extent that the roof caved in on one of the lady's two bathrooms. That would be repaired, we were assured. The same upstairs neighbor for some reason was storing garbage, many large black plastic bags of it, on his balcony, which hung right over her "view." The neighbor on one side of her had opted to use his balcony as a trash dump without even the benefit of black plastic bags, while on the other side lived a paraplegic old lady who had installed heavy metal security bars protecting her balcony from intrusion, although the only way anyone could get to it was by climbing a steep cliff, or else entering from another apartment in the building.

This unsavory arrangement didn't please us, but sure enough somebody took that four-year lease option in less than a month. It was a way to get a foot in the door of home ownership, a start, a break from paying rent, for some first-time buyers whose previous address had been in Tijuana.

The illegal garage house, we called it, because the owners had constructed a huge and completely illegal addition to their garage, doubling the space but unfortunately violating the city laws on minimum "setback." The garage addition loomed into the front yard, ugly and illicit. It didn't go unnoticed, and they faced a grim choice of either tearing the thing down or conducting a house-to-house poll of their neighbors, seeking signatures to qualify for a variance, which would cost at least $2,400.

The house also had a second bedroom add-on, which was built many years earlier without a permit. Because of its antiquity, the sellers believed they could qualify it under a "grandfather" statute, which essentially said that room additions more than 40 years old could be legal by virtue of continuous use.

The house itself was small but well maintained, and the neighborhood pleasant. Across the street was a Mom and Pop delicatessen and corner store, a Greek restaurant, and a coin laundry. These appeared to be mostly for the convenience of neighborhood residents, because they were the only businesses in a zone of densely situated single-family homes and duplexes.

At $114,900, this house was probably the best all around deal in Normal Heights, but nobody would ever buy the place because of that illegal garage. It just scared the dickens out of buyers. The mortgage was called "assumable" on the realtors' printed handout, but a quick phone call to the bank revealed that it was not assumable in any way, and in fact had a balloon cashout due in four years, meaning the sellers could not extend financing on a wraparound.

The sellers were cooperative, however, and agreed to a lease option for a year with a fee of $4,000 and rent of $800 a month, $200 of which was applied to the purchase. It was very tempting, the illegal garage house, and still is.

"We're desperate," the seller said. She explained that in another month they'd have to rent the house out in order to continue paying their own mortgage. This was a case where husband and wife were each in their second marriage and each had a teenage child, so they simply outgrew the small house. Having already moved, they were left with the expense of an empty home in a depressed market. We lowered our offer to $112,500.

Then the agents stepped in, furious that we had actually negotiated with the owner, bypassing their almighty powers of deal making. They demanded reinstatement of the original price. We took our offer off the table. That's where it stands.

Kent's house on Meade Avenue remained to open our eyes. For only $112,900, he offered a house far superior to the illegal garage place, and with no unsightly illegal structures. It was a gorgeous Victorian in spotless condition with light, airy rooms and a completely private backyard. Best of all, Kent's mortgage is an FHA assumable no-qualifying kind!

We couldn't and still can't find anything wrong with this charming house itself, but the location is so unfortunate that we can't bring ourselves to live there. It's on a very busy street. Never mind street, make that a freeway. Meade Avenue in that neighborhood is a broad, busy artery leading to the interstate highway, three lanes across, and roaring with traffic morning through night. Living in the house would be akin to sitting on the Long Island Expressway. Hard to get a good night's sleep.

There was one other location problem—the neighbors. The adjoining property was a three-apartment complex rented out to Vietnamese immigrants who had turned it into a little Ho Chi Minh City resettlement camp. There were many people crammed into those apartments, and true squalor that spilled over onto the sidewalk. You wouldn't exactly go next door to borrow a cup of sugar.

The fact the neighbors are Vietnamese is not, of

course, an allowable objection to the house. The same squalor and congestion would be equally objectionable no matter who the neighbors are. But, although it's wrong and morally despicable, Americans still do discriminate in housing in real, de facto ways. You don't have to be an expert to know that the value of homes in most minority neighborhoods is lower than their white counterparts, and the same is true although less dramatically in Hispanic or Asian areas.

If location is everything, Kent's house suffered a huge loss of value. It's a great place, absolutely delightful, but that busy avenue an those scary neighbors will keep his price rock bottom.

Three fourths of the houses in the downtown port area of Portsmouth, New Hampshire, were vacant and unsellable in the early winter of 1992. This report came from the campaign coverage of Presidential hopefuls jousting for the early New Hampshire primary election in February, amid speculation that the economic depression would be the key issue in the election.

Downtown Portsmouth is gifted with many beautiful original New England homes, made of sturdy wide beams and brick. In the 1970s, a restoration movement saved these homes from the wrecker's ball and slowed the onslaught of modern development. Now, you can have your pick of four-bedroom houses with ample land, some with barns, for about $60,000 each. Yet they stand empty because buyers have disappeared, unemployment is rampant in New Hampshire, and the real estate distress is comparable only to conditions in the 1930s.

How could this be happening to us at the tail end of the twentieth century, when technology and world peace was supposed to heal and feed us all?

Interest rates fall, no credit at all is required, and there's never been an easier time to buy. These things go in cycles, and it's a fair bet that those who buy now will prosper later if they can hold on to the land.

There is only a finite amount of planet Earth on which to live. In real estate, one is said to own the land underground your parcel to the center of the Earth. Right there, in the middle of the planet, some homeowner from China takes over.

Where jobs are scarce, however, homes are cheap. If jobs are really scarce, homes may become free, abandoned, or left to squatters.

As unemployment in San Diego skyrocketed, we wound up getting a tiny, but charming pink stucco cottage in Normal Heights for a song. It has a cute little backyard and a very serviceable garage, old tiles, and charm and banana trees and bird-of-paradise flowers. Even when certain credit problems from the past surfaced on our record, the owner of the property chose to extend his personal trust in us.

So what'll it be? Take your pick. And don't be shy about insisting on your terms. If one seller won't accept your no-credit arrangement, the next one might. It all depends on how badly the owners need to get rid of their property. That, and how well you can present your offer.

Credit is a confidence game, in this respect. The seller needs to believe in your ability to pay. Whatever it takes to inspire that belief is what you need to do. In the case of an FHA or VA assumable mortgage, no confidence is required. Those mortgages are simply and purely available without credit. But in seller financing and most of the other no-credit buying plans described in this book, you need help. You need someone other than a bank or lending institution to extend you a personal kind of credit. A faith. A love. A home.

CHAPTER FIFTEEN

Buy It, You'll Like It

If we did our job well, this book has given you a number of ideas and maybe even inspirations to buy a home without needing credit. It's not only possible, but popular. Even though the "conventional" home purchase requires credit, millions of people have acquired real estate without it.

Remember these main points:

• **Look for an assumable mortgage with no qualifying.** These mortgages are insured by the federal government through the Federal Housing Administration (FHA) and Department of Veterans Affairs (VA). You don't even have to fill out a credit application to assume the payments.

• **Buy directly from the seller, with the "owner will carry" system.** It is profitable and very easy to purchase real estate by paying the mortgage to the previous owner. All you need is a cooperative seller whose own mortgage does *not* have a "Due on Sale" clause.

• **Lease a house with an option to buy it.** That will get you a foot in the door of home ownership, and a part of every rent check you write will go toward your down payment.

• **Save up or otherwise acquire a 30 percent down payment.**   Although it's not a rule, many banks will issue you a mortgage for the remaining 70 percent of the price of the house, even if your credit isn't good, if you come up with a big 30 percent down payment.

• **Acquire title through adverse possession.**   This is tricky and the laws vary from state to state, but you can take over abandoned property through open, hostile, notorious, and continuous use, and eventually gain legal title.

• **Get into an equity sharing partnership.**   Team up with a parent, investor, or friend and buy real estate by sharing equity. You do the work, and make the payments while someone else puts up the down payment and credit for the mortgage.

• **Buy a home in foreclosure.**   Certain foreclosure specialists will sell a home without credit after buying it cheap at auction. Also, homes that are about to go into foreclosure may be available without credit to anyone who will take over the payments.

• **Get a friend or relative to quitclaim to you.**   Buy with a partner, then have that good person deed you his or her portion of the property.

• **Acquire real estate from the elderly or deceased,**   legally and ethically, of course. You can take title through a life estate, "en viager" purchase plan, or probate sale.

• **Look for property in trouble, or real estate that's flawed.**   These "unwanted, desperate, and ugly" properties may be available to you without credit.

• **Be honest, forthright, and fearless in your quest.**   Don't waste your own and others' time looking at houses that you can't afford or that require credit. Make it clear to agents and sellers that you need a no-credit transaction, and you'll find that you *can* indeed succeed!

• **Write if you like it.**   Make your offer in writing. Write to us and let us know your experiences. Write and win, buy without credit and enjoy all the tremendous advantages of owning your own home.

Glossary of Real Estate Terms

Amortization.   A payout schedule of monthly mortgage payments, including principal and interest. The percentage of interest declines, and principal increases, with each payment.

Appraisal.   An estimate of the value of a home, made by a licensed professional inspector who is a disinterested party, that is not under any obligation to either seller or buyer.

"As is."   A condition set by the seller that states that he or she will not be responsible for any defects in the property.

Assessment.   An official ruling of the value of a home, made by a local government agency (usually the county) for the purpose of calculating taxes on the property.

Assumable mortgage.   A mortgage loan that the buyer can take over from the seller, making the same payments over the same term.

Balloon payment.   A payment due on a specific date that cashes the seller out of the entire mortgage balance owed.

Closing costs.   Expenses paid to the escrow holder for the service of handling the home sale transaction.

Condominium, condo.   A private living unit located in a multi-unit complex, such as an apartment or townhome. The condo is individually owned, but the complex has common areas used by all the owners.

Contract. A written agreement between two parties for the sale of property.

Credit report. A report on an individual's debts and history of making payments, compiled by a credit bureau and available to creditors.

Deed (or Title). A written, official declaration that transfers legal ownership of real estate.

Default. The failure to make mortgage payments when due, leading to repossession of the property by the mortgage holder.

Earnest money. A deposit paid by a buyer to a seller in evidence of good faith, which is applied to the purchase price.

Easement. A right-of-way, or legal right to use someone else's property.

Equity. The amount or value that the owner holds in property, above the balance owed on the mortgage. The difference between the mortgage owed and the fair market value of the home.

Escrow. A fund and legal documents held by a trust and disbursed to seller and buyer at the successful conclusion of the sale.

FHA. The Federal Housing Administration, an agency of the U.S. government that guarantees (insures) mortgages issued by banks and lenders.

Fixtures. Items in the home that are permanently attached, and included in the sale of the property.

Foreclosure. The act of a lender or mortgage holder repossessing property from an owner who has failed to make payments.

Foundation. The underlying support structure of a house beneath the ground floor, such as poured concrete or a full basement.

HUD. The U.S. Department of Housing and Urban Development.

Interest. A fee paid for the loan of money, calculated as a percentage. Fixed interest rates stay the same, whereas adjustable interest rates fluctuate with the state of the economy.

Judgment. A court decision that establishes a debt owed, and specifies the amount. With a legal judgment, a creditor can then attach funds or real property of a debtor to satisfy the amount owed.

Lease option. A contract between seller and buyer that allows the buyer to rent the home for a specific period of time and monthly rent, with the right to purchase it for a specific price at any time in the length of the agreement.

Listing. A real estate agent or broker's legal right to sell a property.

Market value. The fair price of a home, based on the amounts that comparable homes in the same vicinity have sold for in recent months.

Mortgage. A legal debt for the amount owed on a piece of property, paid by the owner to the mortgage holder, which can be an individual (the seller) or institution (bank, S&L, or mortgage company).

Principal. The amount of money borrowed and owed on a real estate purchase.

Probate. A court proceeding in which the property of a deceased person is distributed to heirs, after court costs are paid. If a person dies without a will (intestate), the probate court will determine who receives the property.

Qualifying. The act of being granted a mortgage based on good credit.

Real estate. Land and buildings, real property.

Septic tank. A private sewage disposal system buried underground near a house, when public or city-managed sewer disposal is not available.

Taxes. An annual sum, or assessment, paid to a government agency and based on the official value of the home.

Time share. A form of ownership in which the buyer has the right to use the premises for a specific number of days per year.

Title. Ownership of real property.

Title insurance. An insurance policy that protects the homeowner in the event that his or her title is defective.

VA. The U.S. Department of Veterans Affairs.

Wraparound mortgage. A loan in which the buyer makes mortgage payments directly to the seller, who in turn continues to make payments on his or her earlier, underlying mortgage.

Index

Adjustable rate
mortgage, 19, 50
Adverse possession, 21,
110–117
Assumable mortgage,
15, 23–31

Ballew, Lynne, 107–
108
Balloon payment, 57
Bank of America, 36

Contract, lease option,
91–96
Contract, private real
estate, 67–71

Due on sale clause, 56,
132

En viager, 22, 145–150
Equity sharing, 21, 37,
118–129

Fixed rate mortgage, 19,
50
Floor plan, 157

Foreclosure, 21, 130–
139

Group purchase, 122–
123

Housing and Urban
Development (HUD),
Dept. of, 50–51
Hui, 122

Intentional
communities, 122

Kroc, Joan, 35

Lease option, 14–15, 20,
84–103
Life estate grant, 147–
148
Location, 151–154

Monterey Peninsula, 33–
34
Morongo Valley, Calif.,
34–37

Mortgage Bankers Assn. of America, 49

Mortgage payment, 19

Mortgage tables, 61–64

Option fee, 15

Quiet title, 114

Quit claim, 140–144

Reverse mortgage, 146–147

Savings and loans, 17, 47

Seller financing, 20, 33, 52–83, 167

Tax advantage, 16, 18, 119–120

Thirty/Seventy Rule, 20, 104–109

Time share, 123–124

Tokai Bank, 107

Utility bills, 155

Veterans Affairs, Dept. of, 30–31

Wraparound mortgage, 56–57, 79, 167

There's an epidemic with 27 million victims. And no visible symptoms.

It's an epidemic of people who can't read.

Believe it or not, 27 million Americans are functionally illiterate, about one adult in five.

The solution to this problem is you... when you join the fight against illiteracy. So call the Coalition for Literacy at toll-free **1-800-228-8813** and volunteer.

Volunteer Against Illiteracy. The only degree you need is a degree of caring.